Praise for *This*

'I greatly admire how Andrea fearlessly shares her recovery journey in the pursuit of serving others. Let her story inspire you to transform and grow.'

GABRIELLE BERNSTEIN, #1 NEW YORK TIMES BESTSELLING AUTHOR OF THE UNIVERSE HAS YOUR BACK

'Andrea is a glorious human being and an inspiring writer – she is going to help so many people with this wonderful, healing book.'

BRYONY GORDON, #1 BESTSELLING AUTHOR AND AWARD-WINNING MENTAL HEALTH CAMPAIGNER

'I know this book will change the lives of so many people. The stories Andrea shares are honest, open and captivating to read, but at the same time full of incredible takeaways that are transformational. That combined with the practical steps she shares makes this book so impactful and one I'll read over and over again.'

CARRIE GREEN, FOUNDER OF THE FEMALE ENTREPRENEUR ASSOCIATION AND AUTHOR OF SHE MEANS BUSINESS

'An inspiring shot in the arm for any woman who wants to thrive and live her best life. It's like sitting down with an honest, kind friend who will champion you through good times and bad.'

SUZY WALKER, EDITOR-IN-CHIEF, PSYCHOLOGIES

'A fantastic self-help double dose of adrenaline and empathy from someone who has challenged herself to the limit and really understands other women.'

VIV GROSKOP, AUTHOR OF HOW TO OWN THE ROOM

this
girl is
on fire ™

this girl is on fire™

How to Live, Learn and Thrive in a Life You Love

ANDREA McLEAN

HAY HOUSE

Carlsbad, California • New York City
London • Sydney • New Delhi

Published in the United Kingdom by:
Hay House UK Ltd, The Sixth Floor, Watson House,
54 Baker Street, London W1U 7BU
Tel: +44 (0)20 3927 7290; Fax: +44 (0)20 3927 7291
www.hayhouse.co.uk

Published in the United States of America by:
Hay House Inc., PO Box 5100, Carlsbad, CA 92018-5100
Tel: (1) 760 431 7695 or (800) 654 5126
Fax: (1) 760 431 6948 or (800) 650 5115; www.hayhouse.com

Published in Australia by:
Hay House Australia Pty Ltd, 18/36 Ralph St, Alexandria NSW 2015
Tel: (61) 2 9669 4299; Fax: (61) 2 9669 4144; www.hayhouse.com.au

Published in India by:
Hay House Publishers India, Muskaan Complex,
Plot No.3, B-2, Vasant Kunj, New Delhi 110 070
Tel: (91) 11 4176 1620; Fax: (91) 11 4176 1630; www.hayhouse.co.in

A catalogue record for this book is available from the British Library.

Tradepaper ISBN: 978-1-78817-512-8
E-book ISBN: 978-1-78817-548-7
Audiobook ISBN: 978-1-78817-554-8

Printed and bound by CPI Group (UK) Ltd, Croydon CR0 4YY

For my family –
you are my world.

Contents

Prologue

S hit happens. Life doesn't always work out the way you planned it. Money stress, relationship troubles, parental worries (about both your kids *and* your parents)... The list is long and varied, and that's just personal stuff. Job insecurity, poor pay, horrible bosses and terrible colleagues are the tip of the iceberg when it comes to work stress.

Life can be hard. Things happen to you that aren't fair. So by all means have a good old rage about it. Cry, bitch to your friends, get it off your chest. And then decide what YOU are going to DO about it – because *doing nothing means that nothing changes*.

There comes a point – and I say this from experience and with love – when you can't just blame everyone and everything else for the mess you're in. No one's saying you should forgive and forget and let anyone off the hook. If you want to use your fury, go for it – even if you're doing it to prove the bastards wrong! That's great, as long as you do something *productive* with it. If your rage lights a fire in your belly, use it as a PUSH to move yourself forwards.

However, I need to tell you now that doing something productive about the things that have gone wrong in your life will mean you can't sit around bitching about them anymore. They'll become *irrelevant* – that was then, this is *now*. But if you can put them behind you and look forwards not back, I promise you that AMAZING THINGS WILL HAPPEN. You'll be horrified that you spent so long wallowing, blaming and being a general sourpuss.

Even the friends you moaned to will likely be relieved at the change in conversation. And if they aren't, they're clearly not happy themselves – misery loves company, and all that. So, give them a copy of this book and wish them well. We all have a friend who moans constantly but does nothing to change their situation. Have you ever thought that maybe that friend is *you?* I know how awful I felt when I realized that it was me...

But what if you *don't* have anything in your life to get over or put aside? What if you *don't* have the fire of rage and injustice to push you forwards? I hear you. Feeling flat, numb, empty, nothingness. It may not have the drama or heat of all-encompassing fury, but it eats away at you all the same. Having no fire left is as soul-destroying as having one that's raging in all the wrong ways. Life can feel overwhelming sometimes: it can be too big, too much, too complicated, too hard. And sometimes you just don't feel strong enough to push.

And that's when you need a PULL. I completely understand this because I've been there too. You need something to pull you towards the light, towards the spark that'll ignite you again. You think that you'll never again feel the warmth of positivity – but *you will*. You think you'll never again feel the glow of satisfaction over something *you* have achieved, no matter how small – but *you will*. You think you can never again feel the heat of passion for life – *your* life – but *you can*.

Fire is one of the most powerful elements on Earth. It can destroy everything if you let it rage; and if you allow your feelings of unfairness, impotence and injustice to burn, they'll ruin *you*. Your core will be black, charred and empty. But harness that fire, use its power, and it'll thaw you, it'll warm you from the inside, and it'll fill you with the energy and strength you need to move forwards. It'll shine its warming orange glow on everything you see, everything you do.

You *can* do this; you can be the change you want to see in your world. Because, and this is what it boils down to, no one can do it but *you*. I *know* you can do it because if I can, anyone can. I'm here to help you, and I'll share everything I've learned on my journey to becoming a Girl On Fire so that you can become one too.

Let's do this together, and I promise you that you'll feel better. You'll feel ON FIRE in all the right ways.

With so much love,

Andrea x

Introduction

'What do you *want*? It can't be this because it isn't working for you. At. All. You're running yourself ragged – getting tied up in knots trying to do everything and be everything – and for what? You're making yourself ill, and I'm worried about you. You need to stop: NOW!'

My friend Donna was rubbing my back as tears of humiliation, embarrassment and, weirdly, relief ran down my cheeks. It was 10 a.m. and I was supposed to be sitting in a make-up chair being made beautiful before hosting the live TV show *Loose Women* in front of millions of viewers. Instead, I was sitting in a make-up chair crying all over make-up artist Donna, who had decided, as friends do, that enough was enough. Someone needed to tell me that I was headed straight for a brick wall.

What Donna said to me that day didn't stop my crash, but her intervention meant that I got help, quickly. I couldn't deny it or try to hide it any longer – I was coming apart at the seams and I desperately needed to do something about it.

The first thing I did when I arrived home after the show was talk to Nick, my husband and co-founder of our website, This Girl Is On Fire. We'd been running the site for a year and had just celebrated its first anniversary. It had started organically as a place where women could find the information they needed about the menopause (following on from my bestselling book *Confessions of a Menopausal Woman*), as well as articles to make them feel better about themselves in general, and had grown into a full-bodied website for *all* women.

Today, the sole aim of the site is to make every woman feel the best she possibly can, at any age. It gives women the tools they need to empower themselves and be their best, in every way. It's something Nick and I love doing, but somehow back then, it'd become *all-consuming*.

I was getting up at 5:30 a.m. to head to the gym before work and listening to go-getting, motivational podcasts telling me to push harder, stay focused, keep going! Quitting is for losers! Every day, these podcasts were making me feel like a failure, as if I couldn't do it; and the fact I was becoming more and more exhausted clearly meant I *was* a loser and I obviously didn't *want it enough*.

I'd arrive at the TV studio at 8:45 a.m. for the morning meeting before going through the routine stresses of hosting a daily live show; then it was on to doing podcasts and press interviews. Later in the day, I'd write articles on my laptop in the back of taxis, or on the train as I headed home, only to spend the evening working on the website, often until the wee hours.

With the exception of dinner and watching the US comedy show *Modern Family* with the kids (nothing prevents that – we've been doing it for ever), every day and every evening was the same. Then I'd get up and do it all again. And again. And again. I'd been doing that for a year, all whilst promoting my latest book, writing up and pitching a new book, putting together a theatre tour and being a wife and mum.

Nick and I had forgotten to do the very thing that our website told people to do – enjoy the journey rather than blindly pushing for the top. Even though we saw that advice every day in the words of our wedding song, Miley Cyrus's 'The Climb', which are printed and framed in our kitchen.

It doesn't sound like much, and trust me, I know how lucky I am to be living this life. But here's the thing: it doesn't matter what your 'it' is, if what you're doing is making you ill. I'll say that again: *it doesn't matter what your 'it' is, if what you're doing is making you ill.*

Your 'it' may be the stress of being a mum to young children, or a carer to elderly parents; it may be the strain of trying to find your first job, or being promoted to a role you don't think you're capable of doing; it could be being a wife to a husband who doesn't 'see' you any more, or being a husband to a wife who doesn't listen to you any more... It doesn't matter what your 'it' is, if it's making you ill.

Something's gotta give. And usually the first message that something isn't working comes not from the head but from the body. You feel like shit. In pain. Tired beyond belief. Depressed. Anxious. Scared. Angry.

None of these are great words, are they? As I realized when Donna pointed out what was blindingly obvious to everyone but me: I was heading straight for burnout from trying to do things that weren't sitting right with me. I was trying to pretend to myself, and to everyone around me, that everything was *awesome*. That I could handle it all, and that I felt 100 per cent comfortable with the goals I'd set. (*Spoiler alert*: I didn't believe I could do any of them.)

Who the hell did I think I was, saying I could stand on a stage in front of an audience and tell them how to be awesome when I felt so far from that myself? I was a fraud, and it was only a matter of time before everyone saw it. And then I would (quite rightly) be laughed out of town like the failure I was.

I *know*, this is Imposter Syndrome and there are a thousand books on it and a trillion articles, and everyone's got it. This isn't a book about Imposter Syndrome, though: this is a book about recognizing that you're *just existing* in life: getting by and putting one foot in front of the other to survive. We all do it, and we've all done it, but you *can* change things so that you at least get some kind of pleasure out of it. You may not be able to improve your circumstances right away, but you *can* change the way you look at them – and that change of perception is vital if you're going to enjoy this one life we're all given.

This is a book about figuring out just *what* it is that you actually want in life; it's about being brave enough to say it out loud and go get it, and about feeling good while you're doing it. All any of us want is not to mess up this one shot we're given. This really is it. Sometimes, knowing that is enough to make us want to stay indoors and do nothing but watch Netflix until our eyes melt, because we're too scared to try anything in case we fail or it hurts. In which case, to paraphrase J.K. Rowling, we live so cautiously for fear of failing that we end up failing by default.

All of us need to learn to LIVE in the life we've got. The one we were born into. So, how do we make the best of what we're given, and use that to get more? We do it by LEARNING – about ourselves, about what gets our blood pumping and our eyes shining and makes us love what we're doing so much that we wish the days were longer so we could keep doing it. And once we learn that, we'll THRIVE, and love the life we're living. Because *that's* what it's all about.

That's what I wanted. Here's how I got it, and how you can, too.

PART I

Live

CHAPTER 1

Walking through Fire

M any of you in the UK will know me from my 25 years on your screens as a breakfast TV presenter and a host of the daily live talk show *Loose Women*. You've probably read magazine and newspaper articles about me, and you may have seen me interviewed on various TV shows. No doubt you have an opinion of me, good or bad, based on these, and that's totally fine: I do the same with people I see on TV or in the movies.

But how much do we *really* know about anyone? In my case, there's much more to know, and for the very first time, I want to lay myself open and bare to you about my life. Why? Because this is a book about learning to live, learning to love your life, and learning how to thrive, and if I'm going to help you do any of these things it's vital that you know just how far I've come on my journey to loving the life I have now. In this book you'll learn everything that I've learned; you'll see that anything can be overcome; and you'll know that if I can do it, so can you.

For many reasons, I'll have to talk around certain details of my personal life to respect the privacy of those involved. As you journey through my life and my experiences, it'll become clear to you why I've taken these steps. But first, let me take you back in time – to when I met the boy who'd become my first love.

Falling in Love

I was 17 years old and starting a new school for the ninth time because of my father's job – this one was in Cheshire, in the north of England. I'd had to sign in a day earlier than the rest of the year 13s because the teachers were putting pressure on me to drop a year. (I was, however, *determined* not to start year 12 again just because the subjects I'd studied at my previous school were different and I was way behind the rest of the students in my year. I stuck to my guns and did two years' worth of academics in two months; I asked teachers for extra tuition and stayed behind every day to make sure I caught up with everyone else.)

Anyway, when I went into school on the second day, romance was the *last* thing on my mind. I'd been told about this boy who was the hottest guy in school – apparently *everyone* fancied him! I'd shrugged it off – it was of no interest to me, and he'd *definitely* not be interested in my spotty face. I was very used to being last on the list on that score.

That morning a few kind girls took me under their wing and introduced me to the rest of the seniors. Suddenly, there was a commotion in the corner: a boy was holding court, telling his friends about some crazy thing he'd been up to over the summer; he had them all laughing. The girls saw me looking over, and one said: 'Oh, him? Stay away from him, he really fancies himself.' Then, as if sensing we were talking about him, the boy turned around. And I fell in love *right there and then*.

I'll skip the details, but if you were a teenager in the 1980s you'll understand the power of seeing a teenage boy who looked like Mel Gibson and Tom Cruise rolled into one. I didn't stand a chance. Suffice it to say, the boy didn't fall in love with *me* at first sight – in fact, he barely registered my presence. So I sat behind him in geography lessons, staring at his beautiful hair. It was geography that brought us together, though, because we were paired up to do a project. The work itself went okay, apart from the fact he was grumpy that I got better marks for it than he did.

We got to know each other, and I saw another side to him – the one behind the confident swagger. Like me, he'd moved around a lot with his family and he understood how hard it was. But while I'd quietly tried to fit in, he'd gone the other way: he'd become the biggest party animal and occasionally could be a bit spiky. I *know*: it was straight out of a teen movie. He asked me out on a date while we were on our lunch break from our Saturday jobs – I worked in a shoe shop, he worked in a furniture store. He picked me up in his mother's Mini, Van Halen blaring from the speakers.

That first date went well and I found myself with my first serious boyfriend at the same time I needed to focus on my school work. I had *one goal* while I was at this school: to pass my exams, get the grades I needed for university and then leave home. I'd had enough of relocating every few years – by the time I was 17 my family had moved countries six times; we'd lived in Trinidad in the Caribbean, the Philippines, Scotland and England, going back and forth between them. I was sick of moving, of always being the new person at school and elsewhere, of trying to fit in. I wanted my life to be on *my* terms, to make my own decisions, to move when I wanted to.

So I put my head down and got the grades I needed to go to college. They weren't as good as they could have been if I'd stayed at my previous school, and I wasn't accepted by the top colleges that had previously offered me a place, but they were good enough for others. I found a college I liked, called them to see if they had spaces, and then borrowed my mother's car and drove for hours to sit outside the Head of Department's office to hand in my application in person.

At first, she refused to see me because it would breach protocol – I was supposed to post my application. But I knew that I'd just end up in a pile on her desk with all the others. I felt that she needed to meet me and see how committed I was, so I'd stand out. So I quietly waited... Eventually, reluctantly, she let me into her office. I told her about myself and why I'd applied so late; I explained that whilst I hadn't previously studied History,

Politics and International Relations, I was a very fast learner and determined when I set my mind to it. I got in.

Early Life Lessons

You might be wondering what any of this has to do with romance. Well, the college that accepted me was close to the one my boyfriend was attending, so yes, there had been another motive behind my impassioned pleas to study there. It had a great reputation in my chosen subject *and* it happened to be a short drive away from him. It was a win-win.

My boyfriend and I led very separate lives through college. I loved my three years away, and I thrived because I'd finally made my own choice. I'd arrived there along with everyone else, so I wasn't the new girl – I was just me! He, however, struggled during the first year without his gang of friends, and there were many days and evenings when I'd drop everything to rush over and make him feel better, all the while feeling guilty that I was having so much fun myself. I can see now that the seeds for my later behaviour were being sown right there.

After college I worked in an office to gain experience of the 'real world', even though it wasn't in the field I dreamed of working in. I gave it my all for six months, but the company atmosphere was so toxic, I eventually quit. With hindsight, that terrible first job was the universe telling me there were *way better* things in store for me – and I wouldn't have experienced them if I'd stayed!

I ended up doing three jobs solidly for a year to save money to go travelling around the world – something I would never have done if that first job had worked out. During the day I worked as a temp doing reception work and as a sales assistant in a clothes shop, and at night and weekends, I worked in a bar. While my friends were spending their money as fast as they earned it, I was saving, saving, saving. It wasn't a chore, though: I was constantly planning the places I was going to go, the things I was going to see, and the adventures I was going to have!

My boyfriend and I went backpacking for a year, and it was an incredible experience – we travelled all round India, Southeast Asia, Australia and the USA. But we came back separately; while we were away, he'd decided that he wanted to be free of me. I returned a little earlier than planned because my parents had announced they were heading overseas again and they wanted me home to make sure my younger sister would be okay. After one year away from them, I saw them for just five days before they headed off to Africa.

A month later, my boyfriend returned. Apparently, being on his own hadn't been as much fun as he'd thought it would be, and he wanted me back. I willingly went – establishing a pattern that would be repeated. When we finally went our separate ways many years later, we'd been together for 17 years.

Hindsight gives us all twenty-twenty vision. I see so clearly now that we should never have stayed together, that it could never have worked. I think the reason we did stay together was so that the universe could bring our wonderful son, who was clearly meant to be, into this world. *That was the why*. My ex is now happily remarried and has a new family; he's going great guns with his work and we have a good, if distant, relationship. I'm proud of how well he's doing, and I'm happy that he's found a sense of contentment that he clearly could never have had with me.

I see now that loving someone simply isn't enough to make a relationship work. You can't make someone feel the same way about you as you do about them – your love is never going to be big enough for the two of you.

True love is equal – it comes from both sides – and it lifts us up rather than shuts us down. It doesn't destroy: it builds.

I also see that hindsight can show us *why* we behave in the way we do. All I ever wanted was what my parents have: a long, loving relationship that began when they were teenagers and is still going strong. My parents have a very traditional marriage: my mother's job is to look after my father and that has suited them both very well. But seeing my parents' relationship gave me a skewed view of reality. When I transferred that logic to my own, it didn't work – because my ex and I were different people. I thought that staying together was a sign of strength, of love, and that it would all come good in the end. That may happen in some cases, but it's largely dependent on the two people involved.

In every relationship that followed my first one, a similar pattern emerged in that I thought I could 'make it right'. I can see now that my self-esteem and my sense of self-worth became so low that I was grateful to be in a relationship, for having someone love me. This led me to make decisions based on my heart rather than my head.

At times, the behaviour directed at me was much, much darker than simple disrespect or unrequited love. Behind closed doors I was often afraid, but I felt that was the level of love I *deserved*. So I took it all – smiling in public, tiptoeing on eggshells in private. I tried to make myself small, so I didn't rile. I learned to keep quiet, not to protest, and then to go out and smile, smile, smile…

The Burden of the Past

Those of you who've read my other books will know this part of my story, but there are many reasons why I'm bringing it up again now. The main one comes down to timing, and it all began when I participated in a television programme that would change my life.

In the coming chapters I'll be talking about what happened when I took part in the reality TV series *SAS: Who Dares Wins*. For those of you who aren't familiar with the format of the show, it's an experience in which 'regular' men and women are taken far away from their everyday surroundings, stripped of all their possessions and subjected to the toughest military training on Earth; this involves sleep deprivation, violence, fear, hunger, interrogation and mentally and physically draining challenges in tough terrain.

It's life-changing for many of the people who take part, as they're forced to tear down any mental barriers they've put up to stop them thinking about events in their past. Through the very nature of what they experience, everyone is stripped back to the essence of who and what they are.

When I agreed to take part in the show I knew it would be tough, but I wasn't worried about revealing my 'real' self on camera – I've always been myself on TV so I didn't think I had anything to hide. I went on it to see what I was capable of, mentally and physically: as a woman in her middle years, I was curious about how I'd fare. But I hadn't reckoned on my past coming back to haunt me...

When I set off for Chile in South America to film the show, I had no idea that dark, intensely frightening experiences that I'd kept under lock and key would fly out of me like bats from a cave. *No idea*. When I finished the show and returned home to my normal life, I couldn't get them back in the box again. I tried to suppress my feelings – by pushing them down, working hard, throwing myself into projects that clearly didn't suit me, driving myself into the ground to keep myself from thinking – but the stress of doing so took its toll and I had a breakdown.

My mind stopped thinking clearly and I made terrible decisions. I felt that the world was against me, and my body became overwhelmed by pain and exhaustion. When my friend Donna pulled me to one side that fateful day in the *Loose Women* studio she had no idea that all of this was going on in my head – she just thought I was overworked. My husband Nick knew I was struggling to deal with things, but he didn't realize how bad they'd become. No one did.

When the situation reached its worst point, Nick and I had an argument just before I went away on a work trip for a couple of days. Although he'd been only mildly annoyed with me, I was in such a bad state of mind that it triggered overwhelming anxiety and other negative emotions. Alone in my hotel room, I was suicidal. I felt that Nick couldn't see my side of things at all, and if someone who loved me as much as he did failed to see it, what *was* the point?

I wanted it all to end *right then*. But I didn't want to hurt my children, my family – they'd be so ashamed that I'd been so weak. I lay on the floor of my room and sobbed. Then the next day, I got up, went to work, put on a smile and knocked it out of the park. No one would ever have known.

How could I have done that? How can anyone go from lying on the floor feeling suicidal to going into work the next day? Ask anyone who's been in this situation and I'm sure they'll say the same thing: *shame keeps you smiling*. You don't want anyone to know.

All of this has happened within the past two years, and as you can imagine, it's been an extremely challenging time. It's a strange thing when your past trauma explodes into your present; when you're living it, your only thought is survival and protecting those you love. Once you're out of it, you don't want to look at it again – it's done, it's in the past, so what would be the point?

I can see now how damaging that attitude is: not only to our mental and physical health, but also to the loved ones we surround ourselves with. How are they to know what might be setting us off, unless we tell them? How can we ever move with strength into our future if we don't deal with the weight of our past?

When we're in the midst of trauma, we forget that every new day gives us the opportunity to begin again. Every day starts with the promise of a change for good, with opportunities for us to take, things to be grateful for. I'm grateful that I'm here – that I started again; that I kept going; that I didn't lose my faith in love; and that I believed in a better life.

And I'm grateful that whilst I'll never forget, I'm able to forgive. For anyone's who's experienced abuse, forgiveness is such an important part of the process. In order to move on and heal, a point must be reached where there's release. My release may have come much later, but it's been just as powerful.

I've learned so much through what some might call my mistakes or failings. I don't see them that way – I see them as lessons. I've learned that loving someone doesn't mean they'll love you back in the same way, and you can't change that, no matter how much you wish you could. I've learned that the darkness of others doesn't have to condemn me to a life without light. I've learned that sometimes people let themselves down – they lash out and cause hurt, and when it's over, very often it's both you and them who end up bearing scars.

I wish good things for all the people who've come in and out of my life, and I do so for one reason:

I want to live a life free of pain,
and the only way I can do that
is to let it out and let it go.

Bestselling US author and life and business strategist Tony Robbins does a special thing with those who go to see him at his live events. Hundreds of thousands of people, maybe even millions of them, have done it – to prove to themselves that they're stronger than their fears, that their mind is capable of carrying them beyond their fear of pain and suffering. It's called the fire walk.

Robbins gets everyone to mentally prepare themselves, to psych themselves up to take off their socks and shoes, hold their head high, breathe, focus on what's ahead of them, and then walk across a bed of hot coals! I did the fire walk at one of Tony's events, and I laughed when I got to the other side, my feet a bright pink from the heat. I didn't need to walk over hot coals to prove to myself that I'm stronger than my fears, though – I've walked through fire and come out the other side. And if I can, so can you.

CHAPTER 2

How Do We Know What We Really Want?

When I was 11 I wanted to be a fireman. After a school trip to the local fire station I was excited by the idea of leaping up when the alarm sounded, sliding down that big shiny pole and then racing to the fire engine, pulling on my protective gear and helmet and rushing towards a crisis to save people who needed my help.

When I was 11 I also wanted to be a nun. I'd watched *The Sound of Music* roughly a billion times and had just started at a secondary school that happened to be a convent. I thought the nuns there were awesome. I loved the idea of singing in a choir, learning to play the guitar and eventually falling in love with a handsome but sad widower who didn't realize that what he'd been waiting for to mend his broken heart was me and my guitar. We'd live happily ever after in some place that didn't feature Nazis or war.

(My knowledge of both world history and what a nun actually did was slightly skewed.)

A Resilient Girl

Not long after this I wanted to have a boyfriend. I realized you couldn't be a nun and also date Rob Lowe, so I'm afraid I chose the shallower path in life. Whilst getting a boyfriend didn't happen for a *very* long time, and I've sadly never dated Rob Lowe, it didn't stop me from mooning over posters of pop and film stars like every other teenage girl on the planet – thoughts of wimples and whiskers on kittens slowly fading into dust.

As a teenager, when I wanted something, I thought about what it'd take to get it and then I did that. I really wanted a Madonna-esque outfit, so I saved up the money I earned from working in a shoe shop on Saturdays until I had enough to buy one. It was the same when it came to getting that Saturday job – I wanted money so I went into every shop in our town and asked for a job until I got one. And if I wanted to do something, I wasn't put off if other people poked fun at me. I was never part of the cool gang (or any gang, to be honest) so if I wanted to pursue something, I just went for it, even if I got stick for it.

When I was at secondary school (a different one to the convent, as my family had moved from the sunny Caribbean to not-so-sunny England), I really wanted to start a magazine, so I asked the headmaster if I could. He said yes, so I asked lots of people to write stuff for it and they said yes. I designed the layout and sorted out the printing and after a while we had a school magazine! It was terrible, an abomination, but I didn't care – I'd done it.

At the time, I was being bullied by some horrible girls whose mission was to ensure every day of school was as miserable as possible for me. There I was, wearing jumpers knitted by my granny, with hair cut and permed by my mum and with a face covered in huge, painful acne, so doing something as dull and nerdy as starting a magazine literally handed them ammunition. But I genuinely didn't care. They were picking on me anyway, so what difference could doing what I wanted make to that? It didn't occur to me *not* to do it so they'd leave me alone. And I was right – they'd have just found something else to snarl at me about in the girls' toilets.

Facing Down Life's Dementors

As I got older, that cheerful glow of self-protection faded. Through life's bumps and bruises, and as a result of unhealthy and abusive relationships with people who didn't just chip away at my self-esteem but took pleasure in breaking me down until I didn't believe I was capable or even *worthy* of anything, my mindset changed. For a long time, hope and optimism were replaced by fear and tentativeness. I was afraid to try anything in case it drew attention to me and I was shot down in flames.

I was told to my face, many, many times by someone who supposedly loved me: 'I don't know why you're bothering. Why would anyone want *you*?' If you hear that sort of thing often enough, it drips like acid into your subconscious and corrodes the part of you that believes in yourself.

Even if you're lucky enough *not* to have someone in your life who speaks to you in this way, there are enough outside forces who'll do it for them. Instagram and Facebook are awash with people poised over their phones like ugly Dementors waiting to suck the joy out of us. (That's a Harry Potter reference for those of you wondering what on earth a Dementor is!)

The Dementors in our world may appear human – they may look like other mums at the school gate, colleagues at work, friends we've known forever, even our partners – but inside, they're the same as the Harry Potter version: waiting to sneer, take us down a peg or two, and put us in our place. That place is behind them and below them, and if they have anything to do with it, that's how things should stay.

If you *really* want something you have to brace yourself for the fact that not everyone will be happy for you when you get it. But here's the thing: the people who *are* happy for you will be your biggest cheerleaders. The others? Well, the lesson I've learned in life is that if you have to make yourself small so they can feel big, they're not the sort of people you want around you. Even if you really like them; even if you love them.

I'm not saying you should cut yourself off from friends, family and loved ones who aren't telling you you're fabulous – far from it. But if there's someone in your life who consistently belittles you, then you *have* to do something about it. It could be in a private (and probably awkward, hot and embarrassing) conversation in which you ask them whether, when they say those things, they're aware of how it makes you feel.

Alternatively, and only you know whether this is right for you, it could mean easing yourself away from them. I know that's not easy, especially if it's someone you work with, or a family member, but *doing nothing about it means that nothing will change*. Is that what you want?

Are you who you want to be? Is there more inside you that you don't show because you're embarrassed or nervous about what others think?

What if you fail? What if you're shot down or laughed at? That might happen, or it might not. You won't know unless you TRY.

Be really honest with yourself. No one else knows what our dreams are, and a lot of the time we talk ourselves out of pursuing them because we're so afraid of how people will react if we say them out loud.

She Who Dares

Before my experience on *SAS: Who Dares Wins* even came about, I'd asked myself the question 'What do I want?' and was in the process of making changes in my life. I'd worked through the things that I didn't want in my life any longer and was finding ways to work towards the things that I did. At that exact moment, *SAS* appeared out of nowhere. I see now that this wasn't a coincidence or a chance offering. I genuinely believe that the universe decided that this was an experience I needed to have to help me grow, so it gave it to me. I certainly wouldn't have gone looking for it!

When the email came through asking if I'd like to take part, for free, in a celebrity edition of *SAS: Who Dares Wins* to raise money for the charity Stand Up To Cancer, my first reaction was a resounding 'No!' I'd happily do other things for such a great cause, but that? No way!

I turned the offer down and put it out of my mind. But the team came back and asked me again. I still said no. They came back and asked again. This time, I stopped and thought about it. I've been offered the chance to take part in lots of crazy shows in my time and if they haven't felt right for me I've turned them down. The producers of those shows have never come back to ask a second time, let alone three times. Maybe I should reconsider taking part in *SAS*, I thought. Maybe there was a reason *why* I should do it.

I clicked on the link they'd sent and watched an episode of a previous edition of the show, which had been filmed in Morocco. The recruits (as I later discovered the participants are called) were being asked to fall backwards from a great height into water, to fight each other, to trek across hills wearing heavy rucksacks, to cope with interrogation and being screamed at by the men in charge.

I asked myself how I felt watching this. Horrified? Frightened? Or *excited*? I realized there *was* a small glow of excitement in my belly as the episode unfurled. A little voice in my head asked: *What if* you *could do that*?

Let me get this straight right now – I'm *no* G.I. Jane. Yes, I like being fit, but to my own level and in the comfort of a gym. Yes, I like having a personal trainer encourage me to push myself further, to work harder, and be stronger. And I get a buzz from beating my own personal bests, from surpassing what I thought I could lift or hit. But, importantly: I'm not a trekking with a tent on my back, washing in rivers, pooing in the woods kind of girl.

So why would I want to do this show?

Because it was an incredible opportunity to try something different; because I was curious about how I'd cope with it, about how far I could go; and because there seemed to be a reason for me to go that I couldn't yet see.

**Sometimes you just have to trust
there's a lesson to be learned
from doing something, even if
you don't yet know what it is.**

What did I hope to gain from it?

I thought deeply about this. Other than the obvious fact of trying something different and people seeing me in a different light, what did I *want* from it? I realized that I wanted the chance to see what I'm capable of. I realized that we all push ourselves to our limits, but these limits are self-imposed. So how far can we go, and what are we *really* capable of achieving, when these limits are set by others who want us to push way beyond what we think we can handle?

I was very aware that I'd be one of the most mature recruits – what I didn't realize was that I was the oldest participant *ever*. I was 49, and most recruits are in their 20s and 30s, so I knew I'd probably not be as strong or as fast as them. That didn't bother me, though, because I wasn't out to win – I was out to see how far I could go personally. As a middle-aged woman, I wanted to show that just because we're halfway through, it doesn't mean we're halfway *done*.

I said yes.

Ten days later I was on a flight to Chile. I hadn't been told where I was going until I arrived at the airport, but the fact that I hadn't needed many travel inoculations was a sign that it wouldn't be a tropical country. I figured after Morocco they'd want to do something different – and therefore it had to be somewhere cold.

Finding Courage

It was. After landing, we drove for hours up into the Andes Mountains. Then we were given just a few days to settle in and acclimatize to the altitude and the biting cold. None of us were able to relax; we were on edge and mentally braced day and night for being abducted – we knew it would happen suddenly and without warning.

One night, our belongings were taken away from us, including mobile phones. Carrying just a small rucksack of essentials (a washbag and a change of clothes), we were taken to an abandoned hotel miles from anywhere, split up and sent to sleep alone in cold, unloved chalets. I checked every door and window in mine, locked the ones that were open, wedged a chair under the bedroom door handle and slept fitfully in my clothes. It was no different from when I was a reporter on breakfast TV and had to sleep in some pretty hideous, scary places!

The next morning, I was woken by a banging on the door; it was 6 a.m. and pitch-black. I was told to assemble for breakfast, so I brushed my teeth and washed my face in the cold water and joined the other recruits. We were quiet, sensing that this was it. I ate what my nerves could stomach and joined the others in the minivan. A few hours later, the driver slowly made his way down a steep dirt track in the middle of nowhere and stopped the van. We were told to get out and walk down to the edge of a lake. A film crew was waiting for us. Suddenly it was real.

We were instructed not to speak to the crew, so we silently allowed ourselves to be mic'd up with waterproof sound kits. That meant we'd be getting wet. Very wet. Two long, thin open boats pulled up, piloted by Chilean men sitting stony-faced at the back steering outboard motors. We were told which boats to get into, and to sit on the floor. Black cotton bags were fitted over our heads.

Then another boat pulled up, and I felt our vessel rock as more people came aboard, without speaking a word. I instinctively knew they were the Directing Staff, or 'DS' as they're known – the SAS team. The boats chugged out into the lake. I heard a drone overhead and figured this must be the opening shot of the series, and that we recruits had little time before it all began in earnest.

When it did, despite knowing it would be intense, my brain exploded with fear and shock. The boat had stopped and I could feel the grind of sand against the bottom. We were roughly hauled to our feet by the SAS men, led to the front of the boat, gripped by the arm and screamed at to 'JUMP!'

I didn't know what I was jumping into or how long a drop it would be, as I couldn't see with the bag over my head. I jumped, bracing myself for a long fall. It was short, and I landed on a sandy beach. A man shoved me and shouted, 'KNEEL!' I knelt in the wet sand. 'Put your hands on the person in front!' he continued. I reached forwards and did so. Nothing had happened, yet I was gripped by a fear so intense I could barely breathe. I kept telling myself: *It's just a TV show, this is what happens – it's not real.* But my heart didn't believe me.

We were hauled to our feet and told to WALK! We did, clinging to the shirt of the person in front. We were ordered to stop and then, one by one, the black hoods were ripped off our heads. As mine was removed, I saw a pair of bright blue eyes glaring at me. It was DS Billy, who stared into my eyes as if he could see my soul and he hated everything he saw. I instinctively looked at the floor, shaking.

We were ordered to turn around, and in that instant a helicopter roared overhead. It hovered high over the lake in front of us, and we watched as a black-clad figure lowered himself out of its open side and onto its feet. He then let go, folded his arms, and fell backwards, landing head-first in the cold, glittering water. It was Ant Middleton, the show's Chief Instructor.

Then DS Foxy and Ollie shouted at us to climb down a ladder, one by one, into the lake, swim out, fully immerse and climb out again. I didn't question why, I just did as I was told. Then I was ordered to run up the hill to the helicopter. By the time I got there

I was soaking wet, freezing cold and out of breath, and my heart was pounding so hard I couldn't think straight.

Ant yelled at me as I got to the chopper, something about being fucking useless and taking too long. Then he was shouting instructions that I couldn't hear over the noise of the helicopter, so I just nodded. He barked at me to get inside. Before my bum had hit the seat the helicopter roared into the sky, veering to one side as it headed over the lake. I was terrified that I was going to fall out before I'd even done anything.

We reached our point and the helicopter hovered around 30 metres (100 feet) above the water's surface. Ant yelled at me to get out. I stood up and gingerly lowered one foot and then the other out of the open space and onto the feet of the chopper, gripping the seat with my fingers as it bounced and jerked in the air.

Ant grabbed my sweatshirt at my chest and continued barking instructions. I could only make out a few words above the noise of the blades and engine, the wind in my ears, my pounding heart... I knew what he wanted me to do, and the last words I made out as I uncurled my grip on the seat were: 'STAY TIGHT! STAY TIGHT!' Then, with a push, he let me go.

I took a deep breath as I fell into the sky. I squeezed my eyes shut, tightened my body... and waited for the smash.

I knew it would hurt when my head hit the water, but the pain was like nothing I've ever experienced. It was like hitting concrete, then falling through it, upside down, the wrong way up, momentum pushing me down into the cold, brown water. The noise exploded in my head and I opened my eyes to see bubbles and light moving away from me. Instinctively, I started to right myself underwater, trying to figure out which way was up and push myself towards it.

I could feel my heavy army boots filling with water and my sweatshirt weighing me down. I waved my arms ahead of me as I kicked, willing my fingers to break through the surface, just to show me I was heading the right way. They did, and with another kick my head burst free and I inhaled a choking, gasping breath.

It was then that the shock from the impact on the side of my face properly hit me, and I choked back tears of pain. I turned my body away from the shore, where I knew the cameras were, and sobbed. It was the quickest cry I've ever had because I knew the helicopter would soon be overhead again and I'd be in trouble if I stayed in one place for too long. So seconds later, I turned and swam to shore, trying to compose myself.

As I pulled myself out of the cold water I saw the other recruits were getting changed. Our own bags were gone, replaced by rucksacks filled with kit and bin bags next to them for our wet clothes. This was the point when everything we owned was taken away from us, and all we had to rely on was two sets of clothing – one of which was about to be pulled on over cold, wet skin. I didn't know what we'd have to do next, but I realized I'd never get warm if I stayed in my soaking sports bra and panties. Dignity took a back seat to practicality as I stripped everything off, even my underwear, despite the dozens of crew filming us, the DS and my fellow recruits. I blocked out my nakedness, focused on what I had to do and did it.

It didn't stop the cold, though, which had got into my bones. My teeth were chattering and I was shaking by the time everyone had completed their jump. Billy overheard me whisper 'so cold' to myself and yelled at me and the others to do push-ups. Lesson learned – keep my mouth shut.

We climbed into a waiting van and drove for hours further into the bleak Andes Mountains to our camp. I have to be brutally honest here and admit that in between the banter and the bonding with all of the lovely people on the bus, I was shivering with cold and dealing quietly with the shock from which my body and brain were reeling. As we pulled up outside the grey tin outbuildings that would be our home, I pulled myself together and reminded myself that this is what I *wanted*.

Changing Life for the Better

There's a reason I've gone into so much detail about my opening experience of *SAS: Who Dares Wins*. It's to show you that knowing what you want in life and going for it doesn't always bring you rewards in a way that you recognize. That doesn't mean those rewards *won't* come, only that you may have to work harder than you anticipated to get them, and they may not happen right away.

But how do we know what we really want in life? You'd think it'd be the easiest thing in the world to nail that down – after all, we spend enough time moaning about how terrible everything is and how much we want it to change. Get any group of women together, and by group I mean any number over one, and they'll soon be sharing stories about how awful things are: how their partner is lazy, their kids are a nightmare, their boss stinks... the list goes on. This is normally done with a laugh, but the context is the same: life isn't working out in they way they'd hoped it would.

It sounds strange, but I bet if you asked any of those women how they'd like their life to change, once they'd got past the point of 'Move in with Bradley Cooper and lose 10 pounds', they'd say they want it to be *better* in some way. We're all different, so our ideas of what 'better' is will be as unique as we are. Our barometers operate on different scales, which is why there's no such thing as a one-size-fits-all solution to finding happiness. But the essence is the same:

We all want to be happy, in our own way, and the key to finding happiness, to feeling it, is figuring out what we want.

The best place to start with finding out what we really want in life is to write it down. So, grab a pen and paper – in fact, you may like to get yourself a notebook that you dedicate to scribbling down things that occur to you as you're reading this book. You can also use it to complete the *Actions*, such as the one below, that appear in most chapters.

▶ LIVE Action
Do What Makes You Happy

1. In your notebook, or on a sheet of paper, jot down the first five things that come into your head when you ask yourself the question 'What makes me happy?' There are no right or wrong answers here – this is all about *you* and what makes *you* happy. You'll be surprised at what comes out.

2. Now write down what you can *do* to make these five things *happen*. Ask yourself how you can incorporate them into your life. If they're already in your life, ask yourself how you can do them more often, so you really feel the benefit of doing what makes you happy.

▲ ▲ ▲

I was asked to do this exercise by a lovely woman called Jessica Cunningham, with whom I was having healing therapy as part of my recovery from my breakdown. We'd made really great progress: I'd gone through some extremely painful moments from my past and was working towards the things I could do to make my present a happier place. I grabbed a blue Post-it note from my desk and jotted down the first five things that came into my head:

1. Walking a dog in nature and feeling his joy

2. Dancing

3. Making my garden beautiful

4. Sitting in sunshine

5. Being near the sea

I then wrote down what I could do to make these things happen more often in my life. It all sounds ridiculously simple, doesn't it? But I can't stress enough the difference it made to realize that so much of what I needed to do to make myself feel better was in my own hands. When you're in a bad place, you often feel as if everything's beyond your control – it's too big, there's nothing you can do about it, it's overwhelming – so you do nothing.

'Walking a Dog in Nature'

The 'dog' response on my list seemingly came out of nowhere, but I understand now just how significant it was. My beautiful dog Jackson was a huge yellow furry ball of love, and not like how a Labradoodle is supposed to be, which was why I'd chosen him. He had straight hair rather than curly, and shed everywhere he went. He was too goofy to train properly, but he had a heart the size of a planet.

Jackson was my boy and he saw me through some of the most difficult times in my life – the ending of my marriage and the start of my new life, just for starters. Simply having him around calmed my soul and walking with him brought me stillness and quiet I couldn't find elsewhere. Whether it was a long walk in the woods that ended with a quiet coffee and him lying happily at my feet (something I did many times on those painful weekends alone without the children after my divorce) or striding out over the hills, watching his ears fly in the wind under a huge expanse of sky, he filled my heart with joy.

When I left for Chile to do *SAS: Who Dares Wins* Jackson had seemed out of sorts – a bit tired and slow and not quite himself – and on the day I left the show, he took a turn for the worse. I'd called home from a small hotel perched on the side of the Andes Mountains. It was 4 a.m. and hours earlier I'd collapsed at the bottom of a cliff face with hypothermia and had been driven away in an ambulance, marking the end of my time on the show. It'd been a gruelling few days and I was mentally overwhelmed and physically exhausted. After the call I peeled off my cold, filthy clothes and crawled into bed for some much-needed sleep.

Hours later, I rang home again and while I was on the phone, Jackson began whimpering. Nick told me he was going to take him to the vets right away. Less than half an hour later Nick called again, sobbing into the phone. Jackson was gone. He had me on speakerphone as he drove home, talking me through what had happened, and then as he walked through the door at home and told the kids. From thousands of miles away, I heard them crying, asking questions. I tried to console them, but there was nothing I could do to comfort them or myself.

Returning home from Chile should have been joyous. I'd pushed myself to my mental and physical limits and survived, and I couldn't wait to see my family again. But as I put the key in the front door, there was no clattering of paws, no big wet nose pushing the door open, no doggy tongue licking my hand before I could get the key out of the lock. It was my routine to shout, 'Hang on, Jackson! Give me a minute! Let me get in the door! Out the way, out the way! Okay, *now* I can cuddle you!' as I dropped my bags and keys onto the kitchen counter and braced myself for his big, heavy body to lean into my legs.

This time, there was nothing. Silence. His bowls and bed were already gone. Nick walked in behind me, put down my suitcase and hugged me as I cried. Anyone who has lost a pet can relate to this, I'm sure; they become part of your family and are loved as one of your tribe. I grieved hard for Jackson, and I know that his death and the timing of it played a big part in my breakdown.

None of the things on my 'what makes me happy' list had anything to do with my career or my ambitions, which is telling. I'd written them down quickly, and yet they aren't the things that I spend my time worrying about and striving towards. They're gentle things that fill my soul with light, and it's only with a lightness of soul that we can achieve anything.

Can we strive when we have a heavy heart? I don't think so. Work and family may distract us, but they don't necessarily give us the happiness that we all really want.

▶ LIVE Action

Figure Out What You Really Want

Do you know what you want from life — whether it's in your career, at home, or anywhere else? Ask yourself this question, and once your heart and mind have the space to respond to it honestly, write it down. You may be surprised at what comes out. You can try asking yourself what you want in a different way, too, to get to the bottom of what you're looking for. Grab your notebook and respond to these questions.

1. Ask yourself: 'If I could change things about myself and my life, what would those changes be?' This question can be a tough one because it requires brutal honesty — something we're not very good at when it comes to ourselves. But remember, no one else will see what you've written: it's only for you.

2. Next, ask yourself, 'Why am I not already making these changes?' Your brain will go into overload here with a million and one explanations as to why, and I'm sure that many of them are valid. Write them all down: is it a lack of time, money or opportunity? Anything that comes into your head.

3. Now be really honest with yourself and ask: 'Are these valid *reasons* for not making the changes necessary to get what I want in life, or are they just *excuses*?' You'll know the answer because your body will tell you.

▲▲▲

Remember: you *asked* for this and you *want* things in your life to change, so you need to answer apparently simple questions like these. But you need to do so *from the heart*. The heart knows when you're kidding yourself and it'll call bullshit if you say what you think you should, rather than your own truth. It'll let you know that *it knows* by making you feel sick, stressed, anxious, overwhelmed and unfulfilled. If you feel any of those things, that's your heart calling you out. So tell the truth.

Reasons vs Excuses

If you find that you've been making *excuses* about not going after what you really want, don't berate yourself – just ask yourself *why* you're doing so. Is it because you don't want it enough to make the sacrifices necessary to get it? If so, that's *fine*! Just accept it and stop beating yourself up.

Here's an example of what I mean. You want a six-pack but you love cake more – that's okay: just accept that you won't have a six-pack and love your belly as it is. There's no point in wanting something, not doing what you need to do to get it, and then beating yourself up for not having it. That's pretty close to the definition of insanity. Make a decision to accept it, stick to that and move on. *Love your decision*.

If, however, you have *reasons* rather than excuses, ask yourself what you can practically *do* to alter the circumstances that are holding you back. If it's a lack of *time*, be honest about how you spend your days. I'm willing to bet you a million pounds that 90 per cent of your time is spent on using your phone. Do you waste hours scrolling through social media when instead you could be working on whatever it is you really want? Be honest. *Really* honest. Do you get sucked into endless WhatsApp group chats because you'd feel guilty if you weren't involved? Do you feel you must instantly answer every email as it lands in your inbox?

Although these activities aren't bad or wrong, they're not the best use of your time. Fortunately, they're among the things in life that can be *changed* because you're in *control* of them. *Enjoy* this fact, because changing them can take you one step closer to getting what you want!

The easiest approach is to switch your phone to silent so you don't get hooked on the 'ping' of notifications. You can still check your phone every now and then, but you won't be connected to it 24/7 by an insidious invisible cord that tugs at you every time someone comments on a post or sends you a message. You *don't need* to see these every second of the day. If you panic that your kids or other loved ones will call and you won't hear it, you can change your phone settings so that only their calls ring, and leave it at that. You'll find that not only do you magically have more time in the day, but your brain is also free to think clearly as it's not constantly on alert for that damned 'ping'.

Trust me: this is a game changer. I have my phone permanently on silent, and I leave it in my bag when I'm trying to get work done so I don't even look at it. If a call is that urgent the caller will leave a message and I can get back to them when I'm ready. Yes, when *I'm ready*. It took me years to realize that I don't have to be at the beck and call of other people. My time is precious, and I'll give you a slice of it when it suits me, not you.

If *money* is your reason, then I urge you to go through your bank statements and be brutal about what you're spending your money on. You'll be horrified. I was. I used to hate doing this – I always had a hands-over-eyes and fingers-in-ears approach to my bank statements. As long as what I had coming in scraped over what was going out, I was okay with that.

Then came the moment when there was no room for scraping. When the going out was bigger than the coming in and I had to take control. I went through my statements with a fine-tooth comb and was horrified at how slack I'd become. I'd been paying for apps that I hadn't used in years, quietly giving away £10 here and £20 there. I found an old life insurance policy that should have been cancelled years before – how had I not noticed it?

I cut these unnecessary expenses out of my monthly outgoings and that brought me back into the black. Then I took out some of that reclaimed money every month and put it in a savings account. I figured if I'd not noticed it when it was disappearing, I might as well put it somewhere I could use it on a rainy day. I've had a few rainy days since then and been glad of the money.

Change Starts With You

Time and money can be saved and skills can be achieved – today, the internet gives us for free what we once had to spend *both* time and money on. Keep your senses open to passing comments by friends of people who may be able to help you, or connections to people who are open to guiding you. They *are* there, but you don't always see them when you're buried in a place of not knowing what you want or how to get it. The answers are always available – you just need to be honest with yourself and look out for them.

**Opportunities can be had if you open
your mind to them – if you look for them,
if you ask the universe for them.**

As we've just discussed, figuring out what you want can be a serious business because it means that if you're going to go after it, things in your life will have to change. You realize that now, don't you? And if *you* don't make some changes to your life, no one else will do it for you. *You* have to do it. Not on your own, of course, you can get help, but you'll actually need to *do* something, Otherwise you'll stay exactly where you are: wanting these things that you'll never get because you aren't doing anything about it.

Knowing what you want is key when it comes to finding happiness. Whatever was on your list of five things that make you happy, it's *your* responsibility to incorporate them into your life, no one else's. That may sound scary, but it's a *good thing*. It means that you hold the reins. You can do what you choose. But remember, if you want something you've never had, you've got to do something you've never done. And then you need to keep doing that thing until you get what you want. It's that simple. When it doesn't work, you try another thing, and another, and another, and just keep going.

We *all* want to be seen and heard, valued and loved, liked and respected. Sometimes we just don't realize until we see it written down that *this is* what's been missing in our lives. We don't realize that we've been 'just existing', just getting by, and that we've stopped learning and are definitely not thriving. This is something we'll explore in the next chapter.

You really *can* have everything that you want – you just need to know what it is you're looking for and then learn how to get it. Do this and you'll finally be living a life you LOVE. That's the *only* way you'll *ever* get what you want.

Takeaways to ►LIVE

► Saying 'yes' to opportunities won't automatically make positive changes in our life; these things can take time to reveal themselves, so we need to be patient.

► We must take responsibility for making the changes necessary to get what we want – no one can do it but *us*, and we need to make the *first step*.

► When it comes to getting what we want, we need to make a decision, take action, and then keep taking action. We need to be flexible and realistic – we can alter our plans if we need to, but we have to keep going.

CHAPTER 3

Are You Just Existing?

Does the expression 'just existing' apply to you? Sometimes it's hard to know – we can become so accustomed to the way our life is that we find comfort in our discomfort. A familiarity. It sounds crazy, but we can get so used to feeling stuck, anxious, stressed and unhappy that it becomes our normal.

Even more strangely, any movement away from those feelings can unsettle us. We've strayed into unfamiliar territory and our worried brain kicks in to warn us to return to a pattern of thoughts and behaviour that it's used to.

How to Tell if You're 'Just Existing'

Have a look at the following questions and tick those that apply to you and your life:

Are you…

▶ Getting through the day – getting stuff done because it needs to be done – but without real enjoyment?

▶ Doing everything that needs to be done with simmering, just-beneath-the-surface-so-don't-push-me resentment that things aren't working out in the way you want?

▶ Coping on the outside but panicking on the inside that people will find out that you don't really know what you're doing?

▶ Overwhelmed by all the things you're *supposed* to be doing and feeling like a failure because you're not knocking it out of the park all day, every day?

▶ Wondering how everyone else seems to know what they're doing?

▶ Sensing that you never seem to get *what* you want, get to *where* you want, get *who* you want, or feel *how* you want?

And do you…

▶ Have a deadline for feeling better – do you tell yourself things will be better when…?

▶ Buy stuff in order to make yourself feel happy, but find it doesn't work?

▶ See yourself as a victim? Is everything that's wrong in your life someone else's fault?

▶ Expect things to fail rather than succeed, so you don't bother trying?

▶ Complain all the time but don't actually do anything to change the situation you're in?

▶ Ignore problems until they get out of control – and then feel like a victim because it's easier to wait until everything is a total mess and have others step in and take control of the situation?

If you ticked at least half of these questions then it's fair to say you could do with a little pick-me-up because no one should feel this way. I *know* this because that's how I spent years of my life – getting through, getting by, getting stuff done, but with no real sense of enjoyment. I'd somehow got into the rut of thinking 'I'll be happier when...', and that 'when' was anything from losing that pesky seven pounds around my middle and having more toned arms, to having enough money not to worry about my future; it was 'when' I got another job, 'when' my business turned a corner, 'when' winter was over... you name it, there was always something I was waiting to begin or end before I could feel happy or fulfilled.

We all have our own definition of happiness. For one person, treading water in a relationship, in a job and in day-to-day life will be just fine. If that's you and you're absolutely okay about it, that's awesome! You're thriving in your own way. For another person, working every minute of every waking hour – including making family and home life 'perfect' – means being fired up and feeling great, living off adrenaline and loving the rush. If that's you then you're 'Living Your Best Life', which is apparently what we should all be striving for these days.

I think it's important to point out here that *no one* feels fulfilled all the time. No one. Every hugely successful person you can think of has had their stinker – whether it's that their relationships haven't worked out, or their business has failed, or they've had other painful issues to deal with.

There's no such thing as a perfect life – one without pain, suffering, boredom, irritation.

Any of these will pop up at some time or another. So, the difference between 'just existing' and 'really living' is *balance*.

Really Living vs Just Existing

Before we get started, I need to point out that to me, the whole idea of 'Living Your Best Life' is bullshit. It sounds *exhausting*. It smacks of trying to do and be all the things that Instagram says you're supposed to be doing and being, which if you added them all up, is *completely impossible*.

Even if you're a gazillionaire running an empire from your immaculately clean house with children who tidy up after themselves, a chef who makes all your meals, and a yoga teacher who does house calls, there are not enough hours in the day, or even the year, to fit in all the things you're supposed to do. You'd have to get up before you went to bed – which is ironic because on top of all the 'self-care', 'family care', 'relationship care', 'fitness care', 'beauty care', 'friendship care' and 'work care', you're *also* supposed to be getting a full eight hours of sleep a night. *Every night.*

I don't think I've managed to get a full eight hours for seven nights running since I became a grown-up. Then I started working in breakfast TV and had to get up at 3:30 a.m. Then I had two children. My kids are older now, and instead of waking me up at the crack of dawn to watch *Teletubbies* they keep me up all night worrying about how they're getting home from bars after partying with their friends. That's on top of the usual financial/relationship/friendship/money/what's-the-name-of-that-guy-from-that-film-again chatter that my brain likes to mull over frantically at bedtime.

All of these 'cares' I've mentioned are *really* important, especially the sleep thing. But I don't believe it's possible to have all of these things at the same time, not to the level you're 'supposed' to be doing them. Something's gotta give. But that's okay. Some weeks you *will* manage to grab your eight hours of sleep every night, not touch alcohol or sugar, go to the gym every day, switch your phone off two hours before bedtime to avoid the whole blue light thing – all of which is brilliant.

But other weeks you'll have things to go to in the evening, things to get up for in the morning, colds that stop you from sleeping, kids that wake you up in the night, deadlines that suck the life out of you, family crises that need to be dealt with. All of these things will happen at some point, and they'll knock even the most steadfast schedule-followers off course. That's all okay – it happens, and we just start over again. Isn't that what life's all about? Climbing onto and falling off wagons and starting all over again?

'Just existing' is doing all of those things every day with a numb or heavy heart, and being unable to cope when life throws its curveballs at you. 'Really living' is when you not only manage to face these daily challenges, but also *accept* when it's time to curl into a ball and admit defeat for a while; it's when you stop and ask for help before finding the strength from somewhere to get back up again.

This is an important point: *pausing isn't the same as stopping or giving up.* Pausing is absolutely vital because if you don't pause, you'll either fall over with exhaustion or you won't be looking at where you're going because you're so intensely focused on putting one foot in front of the other. You'll be so *in it* that you won't see whether what you're doing is best for you.

And this is what it comes down to – doing what's best for *you*. You can get all the advice in the world, from friends or books or podcasts or whatever, but only *you* can know whether the way you're living is working for you. It may look awesome to everyone else, but if it isn't working for you, then it's time to have a look around and see what you could be doing differently to make your life happier.

We have a big piece of wood hanging up in our kitchen inscribed with the words: 'Happiness is not a destination, it's a journey.' It's been there for so long that I don't even notice it anymore, but there have been many times over the past few years when I should have taken its advice and stopped waiting for something to happen that'd make me feel better. Because that wood speaks the truth!

Being True to Ourselves

So, it's important to find a balance between 'just existing' and really living, or even *thriving* – which is something we'll be looking at later in this book. But before you rush to that section, here's a question: what was the first thing that came into your mind when you saw the word *thriving*? An incredible body, a beautiful home, a snazzy car, going on amazing holidays, earning millions?

That's not thriving, that's an *advert* for it. That's an ideal that's been pushed on us for so long it's become ingrained in our brain – if we aren't *looking like this* or *owning that* then we aren't thriving. As an ideal it's right up there with 'Living Your Best Life' and I call bullshit on it. Most of those things are stuff you can buy that makes someone else a lot of money. Before you can thrive in the future, it's vital to start loving the life you're living *now*.

Take a look at your behaviour – the things you do will make it pretty apparent whether you're just existing or living in alignment with your values, your beliefs and your personality. In other words, being your true, authentic self.

Ask yourself the following questions:

► Do you justify your own behaviour? If you have to explain away the reasons why you do or don't do something, are you doing so for yourself or for others? Most of the time, we give ourselves a justification for behaving in a certain way (I'm tired, I'm stressed, I'm hungry), or not doing certain things (I applied for a job a year ago and it didn't get me anywhere, so what's the point?) Be honest! Do you just *not want to do* something? Are you afraid of change? What's the *real* reason?

► Do you have that horrible twisted feeling in your stomach that something isn't right, but choose to ignore it? That's a red flag right there!

▶ Do you follow through on what you've said you're going to do? Or do you constantly give up on yourself? Or put things off until a better time, which never comes? If you really, really want to do something, you know deep down that you'll do it. So just be honest – you must be signing up for something that doesn't sit with you, otherwise you'd get the damn thing done.

▶ Do you live amid chaos and drama that you bring upon yourself? Be totally honest with yourself here. I know it's easy to blame everyone and everything else, but come on: do you get a kick out of the attention, the hysteria, the fuss? There's a simple reason why you do this: creating a distracting drama elsewhere, either about yourself or someone else, stops you thinking about what's going on in your own life and how unhappy you are. And don't think you're getting away with it either – your body knows, and so does everyone else.

What does it do to us emotionally, physically and mentally when we aren't living life in a way that works best for us? When we're trying to be something we're not? Are *you* being your true, authentic self? Do you feel joy and freedom, or unhappiness and constriction? Your body will tell you whether you're living in alignment with your true self or not; listen to what it's saying to you. The following *Action* is a simple way to test this.

▶LIVE Action

Rediscover Your True Self

Think of a time in your life when you felt as if you were being your true self — when you were doing something that absolutely tied in with your core beliefs, your values, your personality. What was it? It can be anything — related to work or in your personal life. Now ask yourself these questions and write your response in your notebook or on a sheet of paper:

~ How did doing that thing make you *feel*? How did it *align* with you? What did you *get out of doing it*?

~ How does it make you feel *right now*, thinking about that time, doing that thing, being that person?

Living in alignment with your true self will bring feelings of openness, expansion, positivity, lightness and freedom.

Now do the same thing again, but this time think of a time when you were living, working or behaving in a way that did *not* tie in with your core beliefs, your values, your personality.

~ What were you doing? What was the situation? How did it make you feel?

~ How does it make you feel *right now*, thinking about that time, doing that thing, being that person?

If you aren't living in a way that's true to your authentic self, it can make you feel uneasy, disconnected, empty, negative and even physically ill.

▲▲▲

Is the way that you're living your life *right now* aligned with the first part of this *Action* or the second? Don't panic if it's the second. Instead, celebrate – this is great news because you've figured out that your life isn't aligned with *who you are*, at your core, and *that's why* you feel unsettled and out of sorts. You now have a starting point and you have a destination. You've been driving around with no idea where you're headed, or why you're even in the car, so it's no wonder you've not felt right!

Just existing, or being out of alignment with our authentic self, can do much more damage to our body and mind than most of us realize. That knot in your tummy can lead to a stomach ulcer caused by stress; that stiffness in your neck and the migraine you can't shift comes from clenching your teeth; even your teeth themselves can be worn away by night after night of ferocious grinding. The physical manifestations of unhappiness are many and varied and none of them are good for you.

You are you, and no one else can do, or be, or think the way that you do.

There are no rules about how a 'thriving' life should look: the definitions are infinite and as unique as each one of us.

Isn't that exciting? What it means is that only *you* can know whether the way you're living works for you – you'll feel it in your heart and in your body. Your health, your emotions, your mental state: all of these incredible parts of you will send signals to let you know whether you're living a life that feels good to you.

Your parents, your employer, your lover, your friends, all may have your best interests at heart, but you're the only person on this great Earth who truly knows the best way for you to live a life you love. I'm not going to tell you what you need to do to live *one* version of a thriving life – that would be absolutely pointless. I'm here to help you learn the best ways to make those decisions for yourself – to help you thrive in a life *you* love.

Takeaways to ►LIVE

- ► Only *we* can know whether the way we're living is working for us.

- ► The notion of Living Your Best Life is impossible to achieve – no one feels fulfilled *all* of the time.

- ► Our body will tell us whether we're just existing or being our true self – living in alignment with our beliefs and values and doing what makes us happy.

CHAPTER 4

How to Love the Life You're Living

It may seem a little strange that this book has a chapter about loving the life you're living – after all, you're reading it because there are things you want to change. Maybe a few things or maybe a whole lot of things... it doesn't matter. What I'm going to show you now is that you can't change your future if you don't love your present.

Whaaat? Surely it's the 'not loving your present' that's driving you to move forwards, onwards and away from everything you're afraid of or stuck in *right now*? Of *course*, but change isn't going to come if you approach it with resentment, fear or anger. Yes, those things may push you and drive you – they may even be the source of your adrenaline when everything's going wrong – but if you're striving to make positive changes in your life, they won't happen in the way you want them to if they come from a place of negativity.

It took me a *lifetime* to get my head around this; trust me, I thought it made no sense at all. After so many years of living in fear, I'd become used to it. What concerned me more than the fear was *not* feeling afraid – because that meant something was going to happen to take away my happiness. All the time I felt fear I knew where I was and I had something to aim for: getting away from it. There was a familiarity to it.

Breaking Negative Patterns

So many of us find ourselves in awful situations – bad relationships, friends who let us down, money worries, horrible bosses and co-workers – and we can't *believe* that they're happening to us *yet again!* We're good people, we're kind people, so how the hell have we ended up once more being treated like dirt, overlooked and underpaid at work, and taken for granted, or worse, at home?

I'll tell you why: it's because our brain is so used to this happening to us that it looks for it until it finds it and then breathes a sigh of relief. *Ahhh – here comes the put-down. I can relax now...*

It sounds insane, and I didn't believe it at first either. Then I looked back over my life and realized that all I'd been doing was repeating the same patterns over and over again. Subconsciously, I was surrounding myself with people who treated me in a way I was used to being treated, and when they did so, there was such an awful familiarity to it that I accepted it as a matter of course.

Even when I wanted it to stop, I felt powerless to do anything about it. It was what it was.

Is this what *you're* doing? Have a think. Are you repeating negative patterns in your life because you're familiar with them? Think about the things that cause you unhappiness. Have you been here before? Why do you think you keep making choices that take you back? Are you finding comfort in your discomfort? Even if you *don't* think this is what you're doing, at a subconscious level you most likely are.

So, how do you change these negative patterns? The answer is ridiculously simple: you just decide not to behave that way anymore. That's it. Job done. The *unbelievably difficult* part is to keep on doing that – over and over and over and over again. Deciding that you're done with behaving in this way and that from now on you're not going to do it, isn't the end of it – it's the start. Even when you just want to give in, to surrender to how hard everything is and settle into it like a pig in shit, you can't. You have to decide in that moment, right there and then, *I'm not going to think this way*, and then move on.

And if you're thinking: *Whooooah, this sounds like some kind of addiction programme! I'm not an addict – I've never been addicted to anything in my life!'* then you're both right and wrong. We all become addicted to stuff – it's just that a lot of the time we don't recognize that some of what we can't get enough of or can't say no to is mental not physical and it doesn't come from a bottle or a pill.

Let's talk about this. Can you remember what it feels like when you fall in love? It's awesome, right? You can think of nothing else because it's so exciting. You're pumped with adrenaline, you can barely eat, and you can survive without sleep. All you want to do is be with that person, hear from that person, have sex with that person – it consumes you! We all know that the reason for this is because our brain is being flooded with the hormones dopamine and oxytocin, which in a nutshell make us feel incredible.

Who doesn't want to feel like that? It's amazing! And you'd think we'd do *anything* to avoid situations that make us feel the *opposite* of those emotions – frightened, anxious, sick, tense, stressed. But bizarrely, the things that stress us out can release hormones such as cortisol and adrenaline, which, though vitally important to our survival, kind of do the same thing as dopamine and oxytocin – but from a feel-*bad* perspective rather than a feel-*good* one.

So you get wound up, your fight-or-flight response kicks in and your brain starts working overtime to figure out how to get away from this situation. The whirring brain, the sweaty palms, the churning stomach… Sound familiar? Your body certainly thinks so.

Very often, your body can't tell the difference between being excited and being nervous because its responses to both are so similar – only one makes you feel great and the other doesn't. When my teenagers are worried about something at school, I always say to them: 'Your body doesn't know whether it's nervous or excited, so it's "nervous-cited". You just need to tell it that it's excited, to get it on your side and working with you!' I also use this theory on myself if I have a big presentation coming up and I'm feeling wrung out with nerves – it works pretty well.

Body Language and Brain Hooks

In her famous TED talk, US social psychologist Amy Cuddy explains that we can use our body language to change our level of self-confidence. By doing what she calls 'power posing' – which is standing with our hands on our hips and firmly planting our legs and feet on the floor, or standing with our arms outstretched and wide over our head – we can take up more space and *own* it. Psychologically, we're telling ourselves that we don't feel scared, we feel strong; we don't feel nervous, we feel powerful. Our body can fool our brain into thinking: *you know, I think I am capable of doing this!*

As Cuddy says, in terms of confidence, we can fake it until we become it. Our body can make our brain release the chemicals that trigger self-confidence and self-belief. And in the same way, our body language can make us feel timid and small – for example, by looking downwards, hunching our shoulders and double-crossing our legs. Cuddy's book *Presence: Bringing Your Boldest Self to Your Biggest Challenges* is worth a look if you want to dig deeper into finding ways to talk yourself into feeling more confidence.

So, there are situations during which we have high levels of brain and hormone activity – those big spikes that require action such as Amy Cuddy's power poses. But what about the low-level stuff, the day-to-day anxiety and fear that rumbles inside us? I often liken that to being at street level and feeling an underground train running beneath our feet. It produces a strange feeling in the stomach and makes the legs tremble a little; it's so weird to know the train's there underground, doing its own thing, but we don't see it.

That's what underlying tension, fear and anxiety feels like – it's just 'there'. And what happens to something that's just 'there'? We get used to it being there, even if it's something we don't like. It becomes familiar. While the rest of the world is filled with uncertainty because we never know what's coming next, there's comfort in the discomfort of this familiarity – your body recognizes it and knows what it is. Even if it's awful.

That's the physical and chemical reaction, but what about the psychological? This is more complicated. It very often stems from an event early in our childhood that has become a 'hook' in our brain onto which we hang every experience that seems to be similar. These 'hooks' are what we use to learn things. For example, some children pick up things more quickly at school because they've heard about them beforehand at home. They have that *Oh, yes, Mum mentioned that*, or *Dad told me about this*, and whatever the teacher says is placed on that brain 'hook' and stays there as a remembered and supported 'fact'.

The brain does the same thing with *all* experiences, bad ones as well as useful ones. If, when we were little, we were scolded for being a show-off or punished for not being 'good', those experiences became hooks on which, over time, our brain hung other experiences that seemed similar and went on to become more reinforced 'facts'.

The brain is hardwired to try and help us, to tidy up and compartmentalize. However, it doesn't always know the difference between helpful and unhelpful information, so by the time we're adults these 'brain hooks' have become overstuffed cupboards crammed full of experiences which back up and act as reference points to prove that we're right when we think we're weak, stupid, ugly, undeserving and so on. Like a misguided friend, the brain is only trying to help.

Once more, it comes back to fear. The brain is looking out for us all the time, trying to keep us from harm. Therefore, any experience that resonates as something that may cause harm will be flagged up, and the right 'hook' is sought so that we understand what it's trying to warn us about. But sometimes, somewhere along the way, we become so finely tuned to seeking out these unhealthy feelings that it becomes gratifying when we *do* find them.

The brain tells us it's succeeded because it's found what subconsciously we've been looking for. And like a dog that wants a treat for returning a ball, it's happy. We subconsciously seek out the very things that make us unhappy because we've become so used to them they've become our normal.

Let's return to the falling in love analogy. If your experience of relationships – those with colleagues, friends and family as well as romantic partners – has consistently followed a negative pattern, there's usually a reason for it.

So, this all explains how you've got to where you are and why things may have been a little bumpy. But how do you move past this point, as it's clearly causing you pain? You look for different hooks.

Fixating on the Pole

Here's a great analogy I heard at a Tony Robbins event in London. Part of a talk given by one of his guests, it resonated with me with such force that I use it all the time when I'm feeling stuck. I even use it when I'm trying to walk through a crowded street or a train station on my London commute. This may sound strange, but all will become clear:

A man was in a car being driven by his mother. They were on a pretty regular, straight road with nothing around them and were chatting about their lives and the day they were having. Then suddenly, bam! Out of nowhere an animal ran into the road. The mother swerved to avoid hitting it, but in her panic she kept her foot on the accelerator. The man realized she was heading straight for a telephone pole on the other side of the road and so he screamed at her repeatedly: 'You're heading for the pole! Don't hit the pole!' But the woman was transfixed, staring straight at it as she gripped the steering wheel.

As the car got closer and closer to the telephone pole, the man eventually reached over and grabbed the wheel, wrestling it from his mother's grip. He steered the car into the area around the pole and brought it safely to a stop in a field. Shaken but unhurt, the pair sat in the car, stunned at what had just happened. When they finally spoke, the mother said she just couldn't understand why she'd been so transfixed by the slim wooden telephone pole and had kept steering towards it, rather than heading for the huge open space either side of it. After all, when travelling at speed, it's much easier to drive into an open space than it is to aim for a pole!

But her son explained to her that this is what we do in all aspects of our life:

We become so fixated on what we shouldn't do that we can think of nothing else and it becomes what we're drawn to.

In her mind the woman had been saying, *Don't hit the pole!* But her brain locked into the very thing she was telling herself not to do because she'd brought all her attention to it and could focus only on that. Her brain had become fixed onto the *problem rather than the solution.* Even though the solution was way easier to get to.

Shifting Our Line of Vision

When I heard this, it was a huge 'aha' moment! I realized that I do this literally *all the time*. When I'm walking through some of London's busiest underground stations at rush hour, I'm always the one who has to move out of the way of other commuters. This is because I tend to look at people when I'm walking; I don't look at the space *around* them and so I end up – you've guessed it – walking straight towards them. And because I have manners and in general, most commuters do not, I have to dodge out of their way. If I don't, they barge into me, which upsets me and no doubt really annoys them.

I realized with a shock that this is exactly how I deal with problems too. I focus on them, zoom in on them, and then go over and over them until they fill my line of vision and I can't see anything other than the *huge great thing* that's causing the problem. I don't look at the space either side of it.

Do you do this? Do you focus on the problem rather than the solution? What's the 'pole' in your life that you're headed straight towards? And where's the wide-open space either side of it? Do you stand in the shower thinking about the one person at work who really can't stand you, ignoring the 99 per cent of people who think you're fantastic? Do you get stomach-churny over the state of your bank balance while ignoring the fact that you still buy sandwiches you don't even like from the fancy deli, even though you could save a fortune and probably build a nice little savings pot if you were a bit more thoughtful with your debit card?

You're focusing on the problem and not the solution! Focusing on the solution instantly makes you feel better about the situation you're in. This is because you're taking control over something that either you don't like or isn't working for you – or better still, that you really need to get away from. Focusing on a solution gives us a clearer head – it offers us something to aim for rather than the thing we're trying to get away from.

When we're in control of a situation, we're less emotional about it, less angry and fearful. The pole on which we're fixated doesn't fill our line of vision, preventing us from seeing or thinking about anything else. Instead, we're focused on the wide-open spaces either side of it. When you start doing this, you'll begin to realize that the problem you have is never simply the problem – it's your *attitude to the problem*. Attitude is *everything*. If you're constantly looking downwards and inwards, where is your energy going? Downwards and inwards.

If you're looking upwards and outwards – at the bigger picture, the solutions and the possibilities – your energy is directed that way too.

You're focusing on the positive not the negative, even if that positive is a long, long way off. By shifting your line of vision you're making it a possibility. It will *never* be a possibility if you aren't looking for it!

According to Tony Robbins, where focus goes, energy flows. This advice is so straightforward it's ridiculous, but it reminds you to be careful about where your thoughts are heading. Whatever you're thinking about is where all your energy is being directed, and sure as fate, you'll get exactly the thing that you're focusing on – good or bad.

So, how does doing this help you love the life you're living? It helps you to reframe things. It makes you look at things differently. It won't dramatically alter your circumstances – if your worries are finance-related you won't suddenly win the lottery and have all your money woes disappear; however, if you ask for help with your finances, be open about where you need support and start making changes, you'll be focused on the positive outcome of making positive steps to change the situation you're in.

And *that's* what changes your perception of the life you're in: taking charge of a situation rather than simply willing it to change. Wishing that other people or your circumstances were different isn't going to help. At. All. You need to stop being a wimp and letting life push you around. Think about what's within your control and then do it.

The Beauty of Gratitude

I fully appreciate that huge changes won't happen just because you've decided that you want them to be so. But they sure as hell aren't going to change if you do nothing. Doing nothing means that nothing changes – it's that simple. Think about the things that you can do to change the way you look at your life, to make you love it more. Start small – they don't have to be huge. I would start by thinking of all the things I have to be grateful for.

Gratitude is a buzzword at the moment, but I know that some people sneer at the idea. I get it: it's *way* easier to get snarky about all the things that aren't going our way than to feel gratitude for the things that are. There'll always be people who are doing better than us, whose lives seem to be shinier and easier and wealthier and full of what we want. That'll never change. So, get it out of your head right now and instead remember this:

The life you're living right now, even if it feels truly awful, is one that someone else wishes they had. You're living someone else's dream.

Okay, there may be parts of it that they really wouldn't want, but overall, there are huge aspects of your life that another person would love to have. It's humbling to remember this, and it will hopefully stop your internal whining. *You're living someone else's dream.*

What do you have to be grateful for, right now? I'll bet the first thing that popped into your mind was along the lines of: *Huh! Nothing! My job sucks, my partner takes me for granted, my baby hasn't stopped screaming all night, my neighbour is a selfish pig who plays the drums at 3 a.m., I just got caught in the rain and now I smell like a wet dog. And I'm stuck in these clothes all day...*

Gripes like this are perfectly valid. As is the dark stuff that I haven't gone into in detail here but which some of you will have experienced. All these things are valid. But even in those dark times, there will be small daily glimmers of beauty that you can see if you look for them. And you can be grateful for them. Your bed. Your breakfast. Your first cup of coffee. A green traffic light when you're in a rush. A hint of blue sky when it's rained for days on end. A smile from a stranger. The first flower spotted in spring. The joy in your dog's face when you take him for a walk. Those are all things to be grateful for.

When times are really hard, being grateful can be difficult to do. But it's so important and it'll hugely help you feel better about your life in this present moment. Even if you can find only tiny things to be grateful for, write them down, feel them, be thankful for them.

Learning to Love My Life

When I was in my darkest place, none of the things we've explored in this chapter seemed possible. I felt that the whole world was against me, that every problem was huge. I was consumed by the awfulness of it all. I was so busy looking at the pole that I didn't see any space around it at all.

I've already touched on some of my past experiences that resurfaced while I was doing *SAS: Who Dares Wins*. When those memories came rushing back, they didn't just upset me, they changed my whole outlook on the life I was living at the time; even as I returned home and tried to carry on as normal.

No one's life is perfect 100 per cent of the time, and occasionally it can feel like the universe just has it in for you. Every day is filled with new obstacles and things keep going wrong: people in your life become ill or money troubles become so huge they seem insurmountable. Whatever your personal troubles, the universe seems to throw them at you exactly when it feels like you can't take any more.

After doing *SAS: Who Dares Wins*, I mentally went back to a time when emotions of overwhelming fear, anxiety and trauma nearly drowned me. Rationally, I knew I was away from it, that I was free, but I couldn't think of anything else. I knew all the stuff about energy going towards what I was focusing on, about thinking of the space either side of the pole, about positively reframing, about having goals and aiming for them – but nothing made any difference.

I tried to block it out by filling my mind and my time with busyness and business – getting up earlier, working out harder, working harder: pushing, pushing, pushing. But I see now that all of these things were coming from such a negative place and I was focusing on all the wrong things rather than the right ones. I found no joy in anything I was doing: the work I was pushing for, the pitches I was making. I was so consumed by negativity and sadness that I hated it all and blamed everything I was feeling on my situation, the life I was living.

Rather than seeing that *I* was the one in charge of how I looked at things, I let everything take charge of me. I became bitter, angry, resentful, and eventually, exhausted and damn-near friendless. I pushed everyone away with my negative attitude and then resented them for leaving – and I didn't see that I was doing it to myself. *Where focus goes, energy flows.* My energy was frantic, hurt and dark. So I got what I was looking for, and that meant I hated my life.

How did I stop this and learn to love the life I was living? I had a breakdown. It had been brewing for a long time; I can see that now. I was surviving on anti-anxiety medication prescribed by my doctor to try and keep me calm, but my brain and body were whirring with stress.

I could feel my colleagues standing back from me, unsure. I was so far removed from the chilled-out, happy Andrea who always asked how everyone was doing, who listened and engaged, who was interested in everyone's lives, their stories. I couldn't listen; I couldn't take anything in. I couldn't even bear to read the newspapers, filled as they were with negativity and horror that my frayed nerves and traumatized brain couldn't handle.

So I meditated every day and stayed away from the news. I listened to motivational podcasts by people whose lives I wanted to emulate and tried to be more like them and not like me. I said yes to every job going, no matter how small or whether it really benefited me – all to keep my momentum going.

Getting Help

But instead of going upwards I could feel I was spiralling deeper and deeper into myself. I became hyper-sensitive to foods, to moods, to the atmosphere in a room. The things I'd normally let slide, I couldn't: I took them to heart. I was a whirring machine of negativity, making everything worse for myself and not even realizing it.

It all sounds so logical when you're on the outside looking in, but when you're in the thick of it you may not even realize that this is what you're doing. Are *you* wishing for change in your life from a place of anger and negativity? Have a think about what it is that you want to change and why. Write it all down and be honest with your 'why'.

Only one person stepped in to save me from myself – my friend Donna. As I explained earlier, she told me she was worried about me. I tried to shrug it off, but she's as persistent as she is perceptive and she wouldn't let it go. She called me out. And I fell. I can't remember much about that day; other than the fact I somehow did the show and no one watching at home seemed to notice that I was numb, on autopilot. I got home, broke down in tears that seemed to last a lifetime, and told Nick that I needed to stop. I felt like I was short-circuiting. And I see now that I was...

I finally admitted that I needed therapy and began seeing a lovely psychotherapist who helped put me back together again. I'd never had proper therapy before – I'd always tried to cope with things on my own, in my own way. I'd figured I'm a smart enough woman to know the kind of things I'd have to talk about in therapy, so I just looked it up in books and figured it out myself. That's like googling brain surgery and thinking it means you can operate on your own brain. It's not the best idea, especially when you're dealing with post-traumatic stress, as I was.

I felt a sense of shame around having therapy: what would my family think of me? I was supposed to be strong, capable. My parents come from a generation that expects us to 'just deal with things'. To them it's somehow a sign of weakness to have counselling, and it means you aren't robust enough to cope. And what did I have to talk about, anyway? People have been through *way* worse and just got on with it.

Guilt played a huge part in the reason I kept quiet for so long.

I told myself that I should just pull myself together, shut up and crack on. Unfortunately, shutting up leads to cracking up, not cracking on.

Maybe not right away, but somewhere down the line our experiences will rear up and show themselves – nothing stays in the box forever. But why was I going through this at the point when my life was so different, when I was safe? I knew the answer lay in those days in the Andes Mountains in Chile, when all the dark things I'd tried to suppress had been blown into the open and were now alive and prowling around in my body and brain. I was existing in a place of pure fear and adrenaline. Nothing was strong enough to numb it, to slow it down.

Nick and I decided that he should also come to therapy, once I'd had a few sessions, because it was important he understood there were little things he could unwittingly do that would trigger me. I hated even saying that word. Me? Being 'triggered'? For God's sake, how woke. But it was true. Just a look, a tone of voice, one innocent drink too many... things that no one else would notice made my brain explode. I can feel it now, just writing down these words: the prickling of anticipation that something terrible is going to happen.

I said things out loud in my therapist's room that I've never spoken of before or since. The words stuck in my throat; I danced around them, brushed over events with a broad stroke. I was so used to playing things down, to keeping things light, to not wanting to wake the beast... I was frightened to speak the words in case I was punished.

Once I realized I was in a safe place, my body calmed down and the heat receded from my tear-soaked face and my sweat-soaked dress. I was able to hear the therapist's words and not just my thudding heart. I was eventually able to see the terrifying events in my past for what they really were, and look at them neutrally, as if they'd happened to someone else. I felt such sadness that I'd experienced these things. I saw that I hadn't deserved any of them, regardless of what I'd been told and how I'd felt. I saw that I should be proud of myself for being so resilient.

Returning to the Light

Months later, while hosting *Loose Women*, I spoke about the benefits of couples' counselling. I glossed over the reasons Nick and I had sought it, but talked about how healthy it is for couples to learn how to communicate with each other; how they can take into account their current circumstances and the challenges that normal life throws at us, but also consider the things they may have taken with them into their relationship. Through the experience of counselling, they each learn how to be the best partner for the other.

I'd thought it was a positive thing to say, even without explaining why Nick and I had gone, but the press thought otherwise. For months we were subjected to awful front-page headlines about the state of our marriage because we were 'having counselling'. So-called experts were brought in to comment on our relationship – despite never having met or even spoken a word to either of us – and came to the conclusion that we were clearly in trouble.

This is *exactly* why people in the UK are ashamed to talk about having therapy: it's drummed into us that it's a weakness of some kind, a failing, something that only happens as a last resort to try and patch things up. In my case, having therapy *was* a last resort because I couldn't cope with the events of my past any longer. But in terms of couples counselling, it was a fantastic thing to do. Nick and I still refer to it when trying to explain ourselves to each other during the normal day-to-day disagreements that happen in every home.

I believe that we should never stop learning how to be better: in ourselves and in our relationships with other people.

So why should that exclude the person we've chosen to love above all others? Do you think that *you* need help? It could be a friend to talk to or someone professional to guide you. Be honest with yourself – there's no shame in asking for help when you need it. Don't be shy or feel weak or guilty. Ask. That's what they're there for.

During this time, I also saw an energy healer called Marie Reynolds, who helped me overcome the fear that was consuming my body. She cleared energy blockages inside me, which stopped me feeling so weighted down. I also had a number of sessions with Jessica Cunningham – the incredible therapist I mentioned earlier – who helped me by using Cognitive Behavioural Therapy (CBT) and tapping.

These practices helped me to process and release years of damaging and severely limiting beliefs about myself. It was like clearing layer upon layer of filthy silt inside me; I couldn't believe I'd been carrying it around for so long and had still managed to function! They also made me see that even when things seem truly awful – and sometimes things *are* truly awful – there's always a way to find light.

There are always things to be grateful for, even if to begin with they're tiny. For months, my daily gratitude was: 'I'm grateful that I made it through today.' That was it. I still didn't feel right, but I was grateful that I didn't feel as awful as I had previously. When I had a terrible day, my gratitude was: 'I'm grateful that I have the knowledge and experience to know that this will not last forever. This will pass.'

And I started to love the life I was living.

Life is tough sometimes. For all of us. But we can get through it. It doesn't mean that once we do so everything will be awesome and we'll live happily ever after. This isn't a rom-com in which the credits roll at the point where the hero solves a problem and everything works out in the end. Because that bit is never the end: it's just the beginning! Learning to love the life you're living means that you can cope with your shittiest days because you've survived 100 per cent of all the previous shitty days you've ever had – and that's enough to be grateful for.

Takeaways to ▶LIVE

▶ We can't change our future if we don't love our present.

▶ Be grateful – even for the small stuff.

▶ If we're trying to make positive changes in our life, they won't happen in the way we want them to if they come from a place of anger, fear and negativity.

▶ We need to focus on the *solutions* to our problems, not the problems themselves.

▶ We can shift our perception of the life we're in by taking charge of a situation rather than simply willing it to change.

PART II

Learn

CHAPTER 5

The Fear Factor: Why We're Scared of Trying

Deep down, we know that fear stops us from doing certain things. Generally, that's a good thing because otherwise we'd be leaping off cliffs and believing we can jump over speeding cars. Fear is in our brain to protect us – either from ourselves and our own stupidity or from the dangers of the world in which we live.

Chances are, you'll have lived through storms – some worse than others. Some of you are still going through storms, and that's why you're reading this, trying to find some kind of raft to cling to. Hello to you, climb aboard! The thing is, and I have to be really, really honest here, reading this book won't suddenly make all your problems go away, make people treat you better, or lead the job of your dreams to land in your lap.

I still have days when I'm too scared to push myself or jump into the unknown; when I feel overwhelmed by life, consumed by anxiety and so depressed that the world feels like a dark, horrible, pointless place. On those days, getting through a single minute is a challenge. On those days, I feel like I'm drowning on dry land, in full view of the world – only no one can see it. I can't hear what people are saying – nothing goes in and it's all just noise – and my head prickles with pins and needles of stress.

Thankfully, these episodes have become fewer and further apart, and I know that's because I've changed the way I *look* at them. I pull back – I look at the whole view from my windscreen, not just the looming pole. And I also say it out loud: 'I'm feeling a little fragile today.' That way, Nick knows what's happening and is respectful, and *I* know I'm able to slow down for a while without feeling guilty that I'm not pushing as hard as I should. I'm a go-getter, but I now know that I need to go-get some rest every now and then until my head clears!

What's the Worst That Can Happen?

In the build-up to my breakdown, my stress and anxiety became so bad that on one occasion I cried in my car in a supermarket car park because a driver beeped at me for waiting for someone to pull out. The man zoomed past me, shouting and gesticulating, and after I'd parked the car, I switched off the engine and sobbed into my hands. I didn't want to get out but I had things to buy, so I had no choice. I slowly squeezed my way between the cars, pulled up the hood of my coat so I felt invisible and headed into the supermarket.

I got a trolley and started walking up and down the aisles, checking my list and putting things in. I looked like any other shopper, but inside I was in full-blown anxiety mode. I focused on my breath. If I could breathe in and then breathe out again, I'd make it through 6 seconds. If I did it again, I'd make it through 12 seconds. If I did it again, I'd make it through 18 seconds... And eventually I'd survive a minute. And if I managed to survive such an awful minute, then maybe I could survive another one.

I counted my breath again. And again. And again. Ten minutes went by. The prickles eased, and I realized my brain had become distracted by the list, the walking, the counting, the breathing. I didn't feel 'normal', but I felt a hell of a lot better. And I'd survived. Second by second, minute by minute. This is what I do when I feel like I'm going to die of anxiety. I breathe and I count, and then I tell myself that the fact I've survived such an awful few seconds must mean I can survive another awful few seconds, until I don't feel so bad anymore.

Why have I told you this? Well, there are a number of reasons. Firstly, I think it's really important that I'm honest about myself and my life: I'm not some uber-confident woman who waltzed into a job on TV and wrote some bestselling books that somehow qualify me to tell everyone how to be fabulous.

No! I'm a woman who's worked her butt off for 25 years and has survived by being great at her job and a decent human being to work with. (And yes, I hovered over the word 'great' there because I thought it sounded too big-headed. I changed it to 'good', before berating myself for being weak and not taking my own damn advice and changing it back to 'great'.)

I've had moments of absolute confidence in myself and my abilities, and I've had times when I've wondered how the hell I've stayed employed because I'm clearly in over my head and nobody actually wants me. But I've kept going and kept looking forwards. Because what's the worst that can happen?

I've been 'let go' because bosses wanted to 'shake things up a little' and then told I could stay because they couldn't find anyone to take my place. This happened to me three times – in the same job. Why did I stay? Because I liked the job. I've had pay cuts and been sidelined, overlooked and disregarded. And as I've got older, I've realized that these things happened because *I let them.*

Of course, there's not a huge amount you can do if you work for a large company and you're simply a cog in the machine. We're all cogs, really – some are just bigger than others. At least that's the way I've always seen it, which is why I think that every cog is important and should be treated well: it takes only one tiny, tiny wheel to come loose for the whole machine to fall apart.

I didn't have much choice in terms of changing things in the company I worked for, but I could have made changes in *myself.*

Eventually I *did* make these changes because I realized I was surviving rather than thriving. I realize that this is something most of us do – we just *get by*, mainly because we're too scared to speak up in case we lose our job. We need our job to pay the bills, after all. A lot of us keep quiet in our relationships, too, friendships included, because we don't want to rock the boat or seem like a troublemaker – or worse: not to be liked.

If at First You Don't Succeed

Now in my personal life, there are lots of reasons why I didn't speak out, and they all come from people who didn't treat me the way they should have. Fear stopped me from speaking up. At one time in my life, 'Who would want *you*?' was a phrase I heard repeatedly. I hate using the word victim, but after finally having therapy and saying out loud the experiences I've had at the hands of another human, I've acknowledged that in this instance, I was.

I didn't deserve any of the things that happened to me. And rather than keeping myself small and quiet so I don't 'wake the beast', I've learned that I'm not responsible for someone else's abusive behaviour. I don't use that word lightly: it was one I avoided for years for fear of recrimination. It's why I reacted so violently to my *SAS: Who Dares Wins* experience – within micro-seconds of the black bag being whipped off my head and staring into the eyes of a man who seemed to hate my very soul, the box in which I'd placed all my previous traumatic experiences, then buried deep inside and decided never to look at again, flew open…

Overcoming this kind of trauma takes time and I'm still working on it. To be honest, I have good days and bad days. I know I can be triggered easily by a raised voice, a tone, a look, or even just thoughtless behaviour by people around me – these things can send me into a spiral. It's sad really, because I wasn't always like this and I sure as hell don't *want* to be like this. So I work hard at keeping these feelings at bay – by accepting them for what they are and pushing through the fear of pain, repercussion, ridicule or disappointing others.

One thing you need to realize is that you're going to get it wrong many, many times. No one gets what they want in life – at work, at home or wherever – without falling flat on their face, looking and feeling stupid and having to pick themselves up, brush themselves down and start all over again. I know this from first-hand experience; in fact, I'm so experienced at failing it's become my superpower. However, there's another way of looking at it:

The times you get things wrong aren't failures, they're just attempts. They teach you something because the next time you try, you'll do it differently.

Next time, you'll do it another way. And if that fails, you'll try it another way and another and another until it finally works.

Remember, Einstein didn't wake up one morning, discover the theory of relativity before lunch and then receive the Nobel Prize for Physics by teatime. Success in any form takes time and effort. Besides, if you don't get things wrong, how will you know when you're right?

The Expectation of Success

Even if we've mastered the fear of failing, how many of us are dealing with a much bigger terror – disappointing our mum and dad? Although I'm 50 years old the first thing I consider before doing anything is: *What will my parents think?* In my brain, I make decisions based on how my 13-year-old self would feel. *What if they don't like it? What if they get annoyed with me? What if I disappoint them?* For years, every word that came out of my mouth in public was tempered by the thought of what my dad would think if he was listening.

Now to be clear, my parents are lovely people. They're kind and caring and did a great job raising my sister and me. But they're strict – and yes, I did say 'are' not 'were'. There are still boundaries around what behaviour is acceptable and what isn't, especially for me as I'm in the public eye. This means that while my successes are applauded and greeted with smiles by their peers, my failures mean egg on *my parents'* faces, not only mine. I'm very, very aware of this, which makes me extra cautious about *everything*.

It can be crippling because the weight of expectation of success means I'm often terrified of failure. What if I get it wrong? What if I let them down? The fear of disappointing my parents has been part of me for so long, I don't remember a time when it wasn't there. It's something that I have to consciously push against: I'm not *them* – I'm *me*. And while I love them both with all my heart, it's taken me half a century to be brave enough to say out loud: *I know you may not like this, but I'm going to do it anyway.*

Just so you understand what a big deal this is, let me give you some context. Whenever my dad returned home on a break from overseas, and then when he retired and moved back to the UK permanently, he'd text or email me after the show to give me a rundown on what he'd thought of it. This would include things he believed I'd done well, but also everything he felt I'd done wrong. It was horrendous.

My agent at the time did the same thing, so every day as I sat in a taxi on the way home from the studio, my phone would ping and my heart would sink. I had my agent telling me how awful I'd looked – why the hell had I worn that outfit and what had I done to my hair? – and my dad saying that my auntie in Scotland would be furious that I hadn't mentioned something, or that I should have asked the guest this, that or the other.

It was demoralizing. So much so that I let my agent choose my clothes before I went on air – texting them photos of outfits – to avoid being criticized afterwards. And once on air, every word I said, I'd be mentally checking in with my dad. Was it okay to say *that*? And *that*?

Eventually, enough was enough. I got a new agent and started wearing what the hell *I* wanted. And I told my dad, with love, that he had to *stop* doing this because when I'm at work my job isn't to make sure *he's* happy, it's to host a live TV show, keeping a debate running smoothly and to time. Bless him, he genuinely hadn't realized what he was doing; he just thought he was engaging in my career and offering useful feedback. He stopped immediately, and now he lets me do my thing. I know he's really, really proud of me, but that fear of getting it wrong is still there, inside me, waiting...

**What's failure? What's success?
Only you know the answer. You're
the one who sets your limitations,
as well as your goals, no one else.**

In my case, to the outside world I was hosting an award-winning TV show and I was smashing it! But to my mind, I couldn't do anything right because of the words pinging up on my phone, the voices in my ear telling me 'You're not doing it right... you're getting it all wrong,' and the snarls of 'Why would anyone want *you*?'

It's said that success is failure turned inside out, and it is, but it's also much more than that. It's also about *perspective*. I've spoken openly about my struggle with depression and anxiety and I've also written about it in my previous books. In *Confessions of a Good Girl* I looked at my experience of post-natal depression and in *Confessions of a Menopausal Woman* I talked about hormone imbalance after my hysterectomy.

But there are so many reasons why I have anxiety, and they're not only biological. A lot of it has to do with my life experiences and the way I've reacted to them. Some people could have had exactly the same experiences as mine and told everyone around them to stop what they were doing and saying before walking away and never thinking about it again. Others would have crumbled and never got up again.

I did a mixture of the two. I think this is what most of us do: we deal with what life is throwing at us in the best way we can. A lot of the time we're doing whatever we can to avoid feeling scared. That's completely understandable, but consider this: if fear is stopping you from living the life you really want, you're just waiting for it all to end. You're not thriving, let alone loving your life. What a waste!

I lived like this for so long and when I think back on it now, I'm so sad for the woman I was and what she went through. But I'm also extremely proud that I was able to get through it, to find a way out, to just *keep going*.

Unleashing My Demons

I've mentioned the box of memories that flew open while I was doing *SAS: Who Dares Wins*. That was a pivotal moment for me, even though I didn't realize it . At the time it was awful, and I can see now that I was in genuine shock and trauma. Not at what was happening to me on the show, but the emotions that the incident brought back up.

If you watch the show, you'll know that one of its key stages is the fighting – when the recruits are pitted against each other in a boxing bout. This was when I subconsciously relived every moment, every bit of fear, and the emotions I'd suppressed burst out.

After being marched into an abandoned shell of a building and lined up against a wall, we were singled out and made to choose two opponents to fight. *Two.* The universe was protecting me at this point because I was chosen to fight the author and former Conservative MP Louise Mensch alongside the Olympian and England Rugby player Heather Fisher. Heather is strong. And fearless. And used to bashing into people and smashing them up. I'm not.

I thank God it was the two of us against Louise because firstly, Heather would've snapped me in two and secondly, I couldn't bring myself to land a single punch. As we squared up to each other, I looked into Louise's eyes and saw pure fear. She was bravely standing up straight, gloves ready, headguard on and mouthguard in, but she was terrified.

Ant shouted, 'GO!' and Heather smashed Louise in the face. Louise reeled back and then staggered forwards, bravely trying to fight. Smash, another punch. Louise was still standing. I stood beside Heather, uselessly flailing my gloved hands at Louise; I was hoping to hit hard enough that I wouldn't get into trouble, and softly enough that I didn't hurt her. I don't think I landed a single blow. All I could see was her eyes, her terrified eyes, and I was choking with fear. I couldn't breathe and I couldn't hear. She was me... she was me.

Then it was over. We stood against the wall, and I stared at the floor. I couldn't look at anyone – at those fighting or at those waiting. I could hear the sound of the beatings and feel the pain, and it was all I could do to stand still. I wanted to vomit. I wanted to run.

Back in our room there were tears – from those who'd had to hit their friends, from men who'd had to hit women: we all supported each other. Heather and I went on to become firm friends; for all her strength on the pitch and in the 'ring', I instinctively felt that she was one of the most vulnerable people there. Comforting and supporting her took my mind away from how I was feeling within myself. It was the same with my dealings with the young reality TV star Sam Thompson – he couldn't help answering back to the DS and was constantly getting screamed at. I felt so motherly towards him: wanting to protect him from his mistakes and willing him to learn from them.

My behaviour in the fight hadn't gone unnoticed, and that night as we were all climbing exhausted into our army beds, I was called to see the DS. I ran in the dark across the stony ground towards Billy, who ordered me to put my hands against the wall and stand still while a bag was put over my head and blackout goggles were fitted over my eyes. I was led to God knows where, stumbling over rocks and uneven ground, then taken into a room, pushed into a chair, and the bag and goggles removed.

I was at a table with Ant and Ollie facing me. I looked down and waited for them to speak. The silence was long and heavy. Eventually, Ollie said, 'You can look at us, we won't get offended.' I glanced up at them both, then looked down again.

Ant took over, saying: 'You. Are. Fragile… Aren't you?'

I didn't know where he was going with this. I glanced up at him and then looked down again.

These were the bits that were shown on the TV show, wrapped up in a few seconds with emotive music played over the top. What wasn't shown was the verbal pushing I endured before I admitted where my fragility came from. The conversation was brutal, and eventually honest. And it shall stay private. But it gave Ant and Ollie an understanding of why I'd reacted in the way I did, and why years of buried pain flew out of me.

They changed; I could feel the emotion in the room moving from them wanting to break me down to wanting to help me see that I had strength inside. They encouraged me not to be frightened whenever they shouted at me, but instead to feel angry, to push back, to use it as fuel to push through the barriers of mental and physical pain that were to come on the course. Then, with a bark of 'Guard!', the bag and goggles were shoved over my head and Billy led me out of the room.

The tears I'd struggled to hold in choked in my throat; I tried to swallow them down but failed. I started crying, trying to be quiet so I wouldn't make Billy angry. I was frightened about what he'd do to me for being weak, but I couldn't stop. As he led me blindly forward, Billy let go of my outstretched hands and cupped my elbow to help me over the uneven ground. This simple, kind act broke me and the floodgates opened.

Billy stopped, so I stopped, head bent in submission. He gently took the bag and goggles off my head and gave me the tightest bear hug as I cried and cried all over him.

Years of held-in terror – of staying quiet, being strong, not breathing a word – all came out in that moment.

I wailed into his jacket and let him hold me. Eventually I ran out of sobs and it began to pass. Billy gently pushed me away and looked into my tear- and snot-stained face. 'Life is shit,' he said. 'We all have to go through our own shit. But you'll get through this. You will. Okay?' I nodded and looked down.

'Head up, don't let the others see you've been crying,' he added. 'Now fuck off.'

I ran across the courtyard to our dark barracks, but hovered at the doorway; I wasn't ready to face the others. I ran to the toilets – six long-drops at the end of the courtyard that were exposed to the elements and the all-seeing eyes of the DS. I undid my trousers and sat down on the wooden boards to pee, feeling the cold air around my bare bottom. I stared out at the snowy mountains in front of me; it was a clear, cold night and I could see the moon.

In its own strange way, that moment sitting on a freezing latrine, exhausted from released emotion and lack of sleep, was one of the most beautiful I've ever had in my life. We all have pivotal moments like that, when we can decide to push our feelings down and let that weight hold us so we remain stuck in our place of pain forever; or we can decide to keep going – to accept, learn and grow. I decided that night to accept what had happened to me: to learn, to grow and to see where it would take me. I thought that was *all* I needed to do. I thought that having cried it out, it *was* all out. I didn't know then how mistaken I was.

Keeping a Sense of Proportion

The sources of our fear are as unique as we are. Some are extreme, some less so, but that doesn't mean the pain we feel is any less. How that fear manifests itself, however, is common to many of us. Very often it comes down to this: a voice inside us whispers: *I don't deserve to succeed.*

Somewhere along the way, it's been dripped into us that we don't deserve to do well. Whether that's come from a parent, a teacher at school, a spouse, a friend, at some point it's clicked into our brain and stayed there: *You don't deserve this. Get back into your box and stay quiet. You're not smart enough. You're not pretty enough. You're not capable enough. Stop showing off.*

Whatever the voice is saying, it all comes down to the same thing: you don't deserve it. Somehow, we've taken that voice and swapped the 'you' for 'I'. This difference is really important to understand. You didn't start off in life thinking that you couldn't do something or that you didn't deserve it, or that maybe you shouldn't try because someone else might not like it. That came later.

Babies try anything – they grab at life and try to shove it into their mouths with no thought of the consequences. They don't yet know about consequences! Toddlers rush headlong towards everything: open fires, main roads, sharp objects. All the things that give us parents heart attacks and make us hold them tight and warn them of the dangers in life: 'Don't do that, you'll hurt yourself' and 'Watch you don't fall!'

All sensible, important and necessary advice, but as we grow up and move from our parents' side to school and the bigger wide world, those words become less about protecting and more about hurting: 'I don't know why you're trying to do that – you're rubbish' and 'That's so lame.'

We all need to learn how to cope with fear when it happens – because it WILL happen.

As I said earlier, if your fear is of failure, you can see each attempt at something as an opportunity to do it differently. You can of course have your emotional reaction first – cry, scream, shout, sulk, or whatever your go-to response is – but then sit down and draw up a plan for how you're going to try again. That's the difference between people who fail and those who succeed: people who succeed fail *way* more often than those who don't because they keep trying until they get to where they want to be.

Recognize that some fear is normal, rational, or to be expected, and keep your emotions to the level demanded by the situation. Don't make it into something it's not. Remember that things are never as they seem – they're as *we* see them. Choose to see things differently.

The next thing to do is to stop worrying about what everyone else thinks. I say this to my teenagers all the time because they're *consumed* by it. There are two things at play here: one is being liked, which is something we all want, and the other, which is a little darker, is that we don't realize that if we spend our life wanting other people's approval for simply being who and what we are, we're handing ourselves over to them. They're in control of our happiness. Not us.

Isn't that crazy? Surely we should all be in control of our own emotions – not some random stranger on Instagram, or even a partner or friend who constantly tells us we need to wear different trousers because ours don't suit us. Those strangers, those friends, they OWN your ass! Take it back. Take ownership of it.

The Gossiping Brain

We can find inspiration in many places. A while ago I stumbled across something that took me by surprise in how much it inspired me. It was a video clip of Miley Cyrus talking about how scared she'd been before performing at Glastonbury music festival. She'd felt intimidated by the other performers she'd seen smashing it out of the park, being amazing. In her own rock'n'roll way, she summed up the way I try to live *my* life: 'I ask the universe every day: give me something that scares the fuck out of me, and I'm going to fucking do it.'

I had a chat with my 13-year-old recently about what being brave means. I told her that it's easy to do things that don't scare you, but it takes real bravery to try things that you might fail at, those that might make you fall flat on your face. I told her I was proud of her for going on a stage in front of her classmates and us parents and performing, even though she'd been shaking with fear.

I host a live TV show in front of millions of people every week, and despite having done it for two decades, there are still those days when I'm scared I won't get it right. And Miley Cyrus performs in front of gazillions of people, even though she's scared she won't live up to the people she admires. It doesn't matter who we are, what age we are or what we're doing, as Jack Canfield famously said: 'Everything you want is on the other side of fear.'

We're all scared – but isn't it a great feeling when you go ahead, try your hardest and do it anyway?

When, as a teenager, I'd fret about how I looked before leaving the house to go to a school friend's party, my dad would say to me: 'Everyone's going to be too busy thinking about themselves to be looking at *you*!' His tone may have been a little off, and I forgive him for not understanding that the *whole point* of dressing up at that age is so that people *do* look at you, but as an adult I see that he was right. People are *way* more caught up in their own stresses and worries, and yours are of very little concern to them. So don't sweat it. They aren't.

When you're worried about or scared of something, have you ever stopped to really think about it and consider whether it's true or whether you're just gossiping inside your own head? I stop myself short sometimes and ask this question. Oprah talks about this in her book *What I Know For Sure* and I've tried to use it ever since, in my own way. Your brain is an incredible thing, but it's also a hopeless gossip – worse than any of your friends and way worse than any of your frenemies. It'll gossip about you *to your face*, sending you into a tailspin of self-doubt, fear and stress.

So when you next find yourself going round and round in circles, stop, and ask yourself: *Is this actually true? Or is my brain just gossiping?* No prizes for guessing what the answer usually is.

If it *is* actually true and you genuinely have something to worry about or be afraid of, ask yourself this question: 'What can I do about it, or learn from it?' Because sometimes you get things wrong – we all do. But remember: it's not the getting it wrong that's the problem, or the thing to be frightened of – it's what we do or don't do about it.

Sometimes we mess up. We try something that doesn't go as planned. We're thoughtless, or rude, or get swept along with things; and we can be mean. That's okay. Just remember that *you* are in control. If you tried something and it didn't work out, see it as just that – something that didn't work out. If you've got something wrong, swallow your pride, say sorry and do something about it. It's scary, but you can do it. So *do* it.

▶**LEARN** Action

Confront Your Worst Fears

What's the worst that could happen? Let's take a look…

1. Make a list of all the terrible things that could happen at work or in your personal life, or wherever it is that you want to make changes. Dig deep, really go for it: absolute *worst-case scenario* stuff that's right out of your most awful stress dream.

2. Now look at the list. That's the absolute WORST that could happen. It's not good, but now you've seen it written down I bet you can think of ways you could deal with it. Now devise some appropriate responses for each of your worst-case scenarios. In this way, you'll have already faced your worst fears and come up with a solution for them. So, what do you have to be afraid of?

3. Next, write a list of the BEST things that could happen at work or in your personal life. Because if you're going to look at things one way, then you have to balance it out by looking at it the other way.

Somewhere in the middle of your worst- and best-case scenario lists is what will *actually happen*. What's the worst that could happen if you try to change?

▲ ▲ ▲

Overcoming Our Fears

On one of the walls in my home I have a framed quotation. It's one that we see all the time but don't think about too much. Until we *really* think about it, and then it becomes a thing of beauty. It says:

> *What if I fall?*
> *Oh my darling, but what if you fly?*

Doesn't that just sum up life and how we live it?

The author and speaker Gabrielle Bernstein's take on fear is that we're hardwired for it but we can overcome it by choosing not to think fearful thoughts. I've tried to utilize her approach: when I feel myself sliding down into negative thinking, I tell myself that I choose *not* to think like this – whether it's a spiral of 'no one likes me', 'I'm useless', 'I'm never going to get this' or just the internal chatter we all have that makes us feel terrible.

Gabrielle recommends that we simply say: 'I choose not to think this thought' and it magically disappears. And it's true. In her book *The Universe Has Your Back* she points out that we're all starring in our own movie; we're writing our own script and deciding how we see every situation. I think this is such a powerful thing to remember: we don't see things as they really are – we see them as *we* are.

My friend the life coach Pete Cohen says that we need to 'Shut the duck up!' That's how he refers to that quacking voice inside our head that keeps banging on and on about how terrible things are. Remember *that* when things seem to be spiralling out of your control. When you're living in fear and everything seems impossible and too big to fix.

As the spiritual teacher Eckhart Tolle says in his book *Oneness With All Life*: 'The primary cause of unhappiness is never the situation, but your thoughts about it.' On the flip side of this, when I feel myself spiralling into fear and worrying about what *might* happen, I also look into the future and see myself as everything I *want* to become.

I do this while I'm meditating. I like to meditate – it's something I've done for years and it gives me a real feeling of space and peace. It genuinely helps calm my mind. I do different meditations depending on what's happening in my life at the time – sometimes I'm just checking in, grounding myself; other times I need guidance and support because I'm feeling overwhelmed; and other times I'm building my dreams for the future.

I focus on where I see myself living, what I'll look like, how I'll feel, how I'll be dressed, what kind of food I'll eat, how energized I'll feel, how calm and confident I'll be. I can see it all clearly. I know that one day I'll live by the sea, in a house I imagined and sketched when I was a 22-year-old backpacker living in Australia. I found that drawing the other day. I'd completely forgotten about it and there it was – this dream house that I, as a 50-year-old woman, had been fantasizing about. It'd always been in my mind, I just hadn't known it.

When I'm struggling to make a decision I think: *What would my future self do?* I instantly feel the calm, clear head of the woman I've become. She wouldn't panic or stress – she'd make a decision and not worry whether it was right or wrong or how it was going to be judged. It's just a decision. And *I'm* the one making it.

Use whatever works best for you and remember: you may just surprise yourself by reacting in a way you never thought you would. You may be afraid right now, but doing nothing about it means nothing changes. Start small. Accept that most things are out of your control and let it go. Do your bit with the things you can, and let the rest go. You *can* overcome it. And you *will*.

Takeaways to ▶ LEARN

- ▶ We're all afraid of things, but we can work out what we can do to take that fear away.

- ▶ We can ask ourselves whether our fear is real or imagined – are we just 'gossiping' with ourselves and thinking of the worst-case scenario, or do we have a genuine problem we can fix?

▶ It's rational to feel some fear, but we should keep our emotions appropriate to the situation and not make it into something it's not.

▶ We should remember that things are never as they seem – instead, they are as *we see them*. And we can choose to see them differently.

CHAPTER 6

Sometimes It's Not Them, It's You

You won't want to hear what I have to say now – after all, who likes to be told that *they're* the one at fault? But I have to tell you, as a friend, that sometimes, *you* are the one who's holding you back. Not your horrible boss, your lousy ex, your flaky friend or simply life itself. *You.*

There are lots of signs that this is true, but we *choose* not to see them. It's *so much easier* to give ourselves an excuse or to blame other people. We all do it, we know we do it, and we even know *when* we're doing it because even as the words come out of our mouth there's a slightly churny feeling in the pit of our stomach.

That's our conscience doing the gut equivalent of tapping us on the shoulder and saying: *Er, that's not exactly how it happened. Actually it was you who didn't pull your weight, who didn't work quite as hard as you could have, who took your eye off the ball, who became just a tad selfish and self-centred and stopped asking how your partner, friend, whoever it is that's drifted away from you, actually felt about things.*

It's okay to admit that to yourself, even if you can't face saying it out loud to anyone else right now. There's no one else here; it's just us and I completely understand. It's done, it's in the past, and I'm going to keep saying that until it sinks in:

Stop looking backwards and start looking forwards. You can't help what's gone before, but you *are* in control of where you're going.

Once you get your head around this, life becomes so much more positive. And *less* scary, too, because you don't feel as if you're thrashing about and that it's all someone else's fault. You're not lost: you're taking control and taking responsibility for your life. It makes you feel good when you do this; and it makes you feel good when you give yourself goals, plans, objectives, tasks, lists, whatever you want to call them. Because they're reasons to look ahead; they're the light that you work towards. Wouldn't you rather be in the light than in this horrible, dark existence?

So, get out of your own way and stop making excuses.

Which Kind of Friend Are You?

Some of you may be reading this and thinking: *Yeah? Well, you've no idea how hard my life is, I don't have time to sit around writing lists and making plans and dreaming big. I'm stuck here and there's nothing I can do to change it!* If that's you, then you *definitely* need to have a think about how you're looking at things because *everyone* can make changes. Everyone.

We all have our own story to tell. Mine isn't the same as yours, and yours won't be the same as anyone else's; but the thought process behind it is exactly the same. If you want something you've never had, you need to do something you've never done. It'll feel strange, and it may be hard, but if you don't do it, then nothing in your life will change. Nothing.

The place to start is what you're listening to. If you're surrounded by people who don't have a growth mindset, you won't grow as a person either. So be careful who you allow into your head. Gabrielle Bernstein puts it this way: 'I will not let anyone walk through my mind with their dirty feet.' I love the simplicity of this!

I have a friend who's the life and soul of every party and huge amounts of fun; I love her dearly. Even though I have a quiet personality, I enjoy being around her and being part of the energy she brings with her. Our time together always ends in some kind of adventure, and I'm happy to go along for the ride because I'm so naturally cautious and careful that I'd never dare do or say the things she does. I feel carefree by osmosis when I'm with her.

I have a few friends like this, and you'd never put us together. I'm not the one dancing on the tables shouting for more tequila shots, but I'm really happy being around them when they do!

My friend is also an incredible gossip, which makes for hilarious stories. She's a fabulous storyteller – she can spin a yarn that has us all in stitches. But every now and then I have to switch off and step back mentally from this side of her because I feel uncomfortable hearing other people's misfortune being turned into a dinner party tale. I don't like it. I don't get involved with this and she knows not to expect me to – it's like an unspoken rule between us. I'm not the friend who does that thing; I'm the friend to have a laugh *with* people, not the one to laugh *at* them. It's subtle but strong.

Do you get a kick out of it when others mess up? Do you love to spread the word about someone's failure?

If you're this kind of friend, ask yourself what that energy is doing to you and the people around you. Can you be trusted? Why are you doing it? Does it make you feel better about yourself when other people mess up? I know we all have that in us – we can feel a little jolt of relief that someone who appears to have it all figured out is human just like the rest of us. That's normal. But do you relish it? Roll around in it? Spread it about and take pleasure in it? That's not good for you, never mind them.

Over the years my view on friendship has changed. Today, It's more complicated than it used to be, on my part. I know that I don't always let people in too deeply and that I protect myself. It was Nick who pointed out to me that I can be friendly but aloof and that I tend to keep to myself. I think this has happened to me so gradually that I haven't seen it. Yet I understand clearly why I am this way: I moved around a lot when I was younger, and I lost friends through getting divorced not once, but twice.

For two decades I've worked in an industry in which many people are nice to your face and downright Machiavellian behind your back! It's become less painful just to keep a distance rather than let someone in and be disappointed when they reveal their true selves or simply fade away when you've outlived your usefulness. I see that this attitude has come from me, not from others, and it makes me sad to think of the friendships I could have made if I hadn't backed away from some truly lovely people who've reached out to me. In these instances, it most definitely has been me, not them. But I'm more aware of this now and I'm trying to improve!

Friendships come and go for all sorts of reasons. Some are fiery and end with an explosion; others wither on the vine because time, distance and other commitments take precedence. Where do you stand in these and is there anything you can do to change it?

Which Kind of Partner Are You?

I'm asking this question from the perspective of someone who's been married three times – I've experienced heartbreak that would have registered a 10 on the Richter scale! Whether you've been with the same person your whole life; whether you've had many relationships that just never seem to work; or whether you're resolutely single, it takes a strong person to look inwards and think: *What could I have done differently?*

With hindsight I can see that I made many mistakes in my previous relationships. The main one being that I thought the other person wanted the same things I did; I was oblivious to the fact that they clearly didn't. I can see now that what I thought of as 'loving' from my side was viewed as stifling, claustrophobic, irritating from the other. I also thought I could 'fix' someone; I know now that wasn't my responsibility and that the best thing I could have done was walk away.

All relationships are different, but if they're unequal in their intention then they're never going to work. I'm much more aware of this now because of the harsh lessons that my relationships have taught me. When I think back on those relationships, and my reaction to them, I can see there were times when I tried to change how things were to make them how I *wanted* them to be, rather than accept them and walk away.

I didn't realize that I was doing the wrong thing – not at all. I thought that by trying to make things work, I was doing the *proper* thing. Isn't that what women are raised to do – make relationships work? But who decided this, and when was it agreed that it was a 'good thing'? Whilst I absolutely see there were many parts of my relationships that weren't my fault, there were also many things I could have done differently.

Which Kind of Employee Are You?

I'm a strong person, quietly strong, and I've always had self-belief. I just knew I was going to do something extraordinary with my life – that I was destined for a life of adventure and that it would never be dull. I knew I wanted to do incredible things and to travel, write and bring joy. I didn't quite know how, but I knew it would happen. When I was younger, that deeply held knowledge made me less worried about the details because I felt it was my destiny!

I remember talking to the editor of the local newspaper I worked on at the age of 15. I was hanging around, doing stuff for free, asking to sit with seasoned journalists on stories so I could learn from them. The editor asked if I'd found the experience useful, and whether I knew what I wanted to do with it. I told him: 'I'm going to be the youngest ever editor of *Cosmopolitan* magazine!' To me, that magazine was the pinnacle of sophistication and I knew that if I worked for them, I'd have 'made it'. He smiled and wished me luck.

I was 15, living in a small town in the middle of England, and the odds of making it in London as a magazine editor were very much stacked against me. I didn't see it that way at all, though; I just thought: why *not* me?

I wish that attitude could be bottled and drunk, like something from Alice In Wonderland – we'd all be so much better off being able to take a little sip every time we needed it. I find it fascinating when I think back now on my attitude at that time. It's not as if everything was going so amazingly well for me that I just assumed life was a bed of roses waiting to be picked. I'd been moved away from a place I loved (Trinidad in the Caribbean) yet again because of my dad's job and was living in England, where I was seen as a bit of a weirdo because of my strange accent and foreign ways. It was 1984, and a white girl with a black girl's voice was quite the novelty, and not always in a good way. I'd made friends, but they magically melted away when the school bullies (whom I'd antagonized by sticking up for one poor girl in the locker room) appeared.

During this time I was nervous, but I had a resigned acceptance of the fact I was being bullied for sticking up for someone who couldn't do it for herself, and because I was different. I understood why they did it; I reasoned that I must seem so odd to them. But I knew it would end at some point because school would finish and we'd all leave.

So I focused on the things I wanted to happen to me, not the things I didn't. I wanted to be an actress as well as a writer, so

I went to drama club and joined the debating team and all the nerdy things that girls like me did. I wrote constantly, thinking about the day when I'd move to London and write for a magazine for a living

I was focusing on all the right things, not the wrong ones. My energy flowed away from my immediate problems and towards my dream life, so *that* was where I headed. I didn't know it at the time, but the way I thought and behaved 100 per cent led me to the life I have now. I looked for the positives and made decisions with a brave heart and not through fear. I didn't change who I was or how I behaved – I just kept looking ahead. Don't get me wrong: I hated my situation and I was scared and angry, but I knew it would pass.

I'm so thankful that I looked upwards and not down. That I never gave up. I may have changed my direction a little, but I always steered my career ship forwards. Of course, I couldn't have foreseen how my personal life would end up – maybe I should have spent more time with boys and less time with my nose in a book. I'd have been a helluva lot more worldly! But I didn't and I wasn't, and the way I see it, everything happened for a reason. So I accept it: it led me to where I am today, so I'm thankful.

Most of us who go out to work tend to focus on the job we have to do and don't often give much thought to *how* we're doing it. What are we like to work with? What kind of energy are we giving off to the people around us? As I mentioned earlier, at my worst I was a whirl of negative energy, subconsciously looking for anything to justify it. Yes, I did my job and did it well, but what was I like to work with? I shudder to think.

Have a look at your own behaviour. Could there be a reason why opportunities just don't seem to work out for you? Or why you haven't made many work friends? Maybe it's not all down to everyone else...

Reframing Our Thoughts

After my breakdown, I had to completely change the way I felt about work, and also about money, my health and my relationships. I stopped looking at the parts of them that were wrong, that were lacking, and had huge, insurmountable problems. Doing this *totally* changed the way I looked at things. As a result, the situations themselves didn't change but my *perception* of them did. I was able to view them much more clearly and therefore see a way around them. See the space around the pole, if you like.

Once I did that, the solutions presented themselves and it became clear that it wasn't just the problems that were the problem, it was my *attitude* towards them. Even my attitude towards my daily meditations changed. The mantra 'Everything in this moment is exactly as it should be' used to grate on me, and although I'd say it, I wouldn't feel it. Inside I'd be raging: *No, it isn't! I'm unhappy! I'm sick! I hate my life!* I see now that I was trying to wrestle control of these things. I needed to be more Elsa from *Frozen* and Let It Go.

Life coach Pete Cohen has an interesting take on this. In his book *Shut the Duck Up*, which is about quietening the voice that incessantly quacks in our head and makes us think ridiculous negative thoughts, he suggests we ask ourselves, 'Is this situation in my control?' and 'If I were the other person, what might my motive be?' In other words, is this situation or problem about them, or you?

This is fascinating because actually, we don't know. As Pete explains, unless they specifically tell us, we have *no idea* what our friends and family, or anyone else, is thinking, or why they behave in the way they do. So we make up our own stories to suit what we *think* is happening and then we make that our truth.

Don't believe me? Think of one of your friends who *you* think is being a little off with you. You weren't invited out for drinks with the group you normally go with, and you swear this friend is always 'popping round' to see the other girls but not you. They're probably talking about you! In fact, they do seem to be a bit strange with you, and you're sure she looked at you oddly.

Now you're probably on your guard around this friend: not engaging with her, wary, watching your back. Which she picks up on and is now wary around *you*. Which fulfils everything you feared and proves your theory correct. Well done! But have you ever thought that maybe *you're* the one who's bringing this all on yourself? That you've created this story in your own head?

You *could* be right. Maybe she *is* a sneaky two-faced cow going behind your back. But maybe she's not, and you've manifested the whole thing by writing your own story and acting it out. What a horrible thought. What a waste of your time and energy.

Consider what's *actually* happening, rather than what you *think* is happening.

And remember: most people behave badly because they *aren't* thinking rather than because they are. Is the situation you're in *really* awful? Or are you making a drama out of nothing? Will it matter in five minutes' time? By the end of the day? In a week? In a month? In a year? If it won't, it doesn't really matter. Is this situation actually an opportunity to learn something – either about yourself or the situation itself? Sometimes the universe takes us away from what we're trying so hard to get. It puts obstacles in our way that seem really unfair; it blocks our progress and gives us illness, antagonism, hardship.

Stop and think: what are you meant to learn from this situation? Is it to look after yourself better? To pay more attention to the food you eat and your habits? Is it to walk away from a toxic relationship that could never have worked? It's taken me a long time and a lot of hardship and growth to get to the point now where I do look at difficult situations and think *What am I meant to learn from this? What's the real reason this has happened?*

Focus on the Cheerleaders

Remember that you always have a *choice* about the way you react to something. *Always*. Your reaction isn't the *only* option, it's just the first one you have. So think again. How would you choose to react to something if you had the time to consider it? Next time, make a conscious decision to react in *that* way – choose the better option. See humour in it. See irrelevance in it. See whatever you like, as long as it's positive and helpful rather than negative and unhelpful.

There's humour or learning to be had in every situation, even the truly awful ones.

The writer, broadcaster and comedian Viv Groskop talks about overthinking a situation and making it all about *her* in her wonderful book *How to Own the Room*. Viv is an incredible woman – funny, warm and smart. She's an excellent public speaker, but once while making a speech she noticed there was *one* bored and uninterested audience member, and they became the *only* person in the room on whom she could focus.

I've done this myself – once while giving a talk I noticed a woman in the front row who repeatedly looked at her watch. I kept losing my stride, thinking: *Why is she here if she doesn't want to be? Am I that dull?* It hugely put me off. I could feel myself doubting my own words, despite the fact that a few weeks earlier, I'd done a similar talk and had the room roaring with laughter and wiping away tears of emotion. I'd knocked it out of the park.

On this occasion, faced with this one woman, I couldn't concentrate. I ended up doing the whole talk for *her*, trying to win her round. I forgot about the rest of the audience, who *were* listening and enjoying themselves. I know I didn't give my best talk that day, and afterwards I was even more annoyed with myself when the woman joined the queue of people waiting for me to sign copies of my book. It turned out that a friend was supposed to join her and she'd been looking at her watch and wondering where she was, cross that she was missing a great night. It'd had *nothing to do with me*. I vowed never to do that again.

On the flip side, of course there'll be people you encounter who don't like you and who don't want to see you do well. In that case, it absolutely *is* everything to do with them and not you. So take Viv's advice: never focus on the one person who's dragging you down and making you feel unworthy. Focus on your cheerleaders, your champions: they're the ones who are there for you. That one person never was and never will be. So fuck 'em.

Why Our Words Matter

When you're dealing with 'you' and not 'them', be super-vigilant around the words you use to talk to yourself. We all know how important language is and how much we alter it depending on who we're talking to – that's why we don't swear in front of our mum but turn the air blue when telling jokes to our friends!

The language we use when we talk to ourselves, and how we frame the events around us, has a *huge* effect on us psychologically. But we don't even notice it because those words become our norm. Would you talk to a friend the way you talk to yourself? If you did, you wouldn't have many friends left. What a moaning, negative, navel-gazing Mean Girl you are! *I don't know why you're even trying. Everyone's going to laugh at you. No one's going to come. So and so will be there, and you know she hates you...* You know how it goes.

Call that negative voice your 'chimp' (if you've read *The Chimp Paradox* by Professor Steve Peters, you'll know what I'm referring to), your 'inner critic', or your 'duck', as Pete Cohen suggests, as it quacks away incessantly, reminding you of all the things you've got wrong and are going to get wrong, and how much you think everyone else thinks you're getting it wrong.

When times are tough, when every news station and newspaper is revelling in wall-to-wall reporting on every terrible thing that's happening in the world, the words we're surrounded by every minute of the day seep into our subconscious and lodge themselves there. Just think about what that's doing to you – listening to hourly hypothesizing about how truly awful everything is and could be. I'm not saying that we need to walk around with our fingers in our ears, but sticking to the facts rather than the hypothesizing helps our fearful brain focus on those rather than fiction.

And that's just the words we're *listening* to – the words we *say* have just as huge an impact. We all have friends who naturally lean to the dark side and are the Eeyore to everyone else's Tigger. Think of the language they use: things are always a *disaster*; they aren't just upset, they're *devastated* and *furious*; everything is *hopeless*! It's no surprise to learn that these and words like them trigger a response in both their brain and ours.

Think about the words that *you* use – when you're talking to yourself and to others. What kind of state are you talking yourself into rather than out of? You can *choose* the way your mind sees things – choose to see the good or the bad. If there's a problem in your life right now, rather than dwelling on it, think about what it might be trying to teach you. What can you *learn* from it?

We need to really think about the way we talk to ourselves and others – to consider carefully what the language we use means and how we're talking ourselves into *feeling*.

Using the right words can shift our perspective and fill us with love, joy and gratitude.

Think too about what using the right words does to our bodies – we feel lighter, energized, better able to cope. On the other hand, using the wrong words can make us feel angry, depressed and fearful, which releases stress hormones. The brain reacts in the way we've told it to – it goes on guard, ready to protect us from harm. Our fuse is short, we're on edge and we're primed to react! And not in the best way.

When things are tough and scary our natural response is to be afraid and to surround ourselves with people who feel the same way. But by simply changing the words we use around that same situation, we can transform the way we view it.

Have a think about the words *you* use when talking about yourself and a situation, and how much it could benefit you to change them. Are things *really* devastating? Or are they difficult? Why not have a swap around – instead of catastrophizing the negative and minimizing the positive, minimize what's going wrong and maximize what's going right.

Instead of just feeling okay, why not feel *amazing!* I know, I know: every cell in your body is probably recoiling at the thought of such ostentatious cheerfulness, but give it a go. Those little word swaps alone will have an outstanding effect on your psyche.

How much time do you waste wishing things were different and moaning about the state of your life? Feeling sorry for yourself gets you absolutely *nowhere*. For every gripe you have there'll be someone who faced ten times your adversity and overcame it. Of course you can dig in and find reasons why your situation is worse than someone else's, and your resolution may not be exactly the same as theirs. However, even just *accepting* your situation and then working on a way to resolve it puts you a million light years ahead of those who do nothing.

Everyone's difficulties are unique, even if there are threads of similarities that bind us together. But the one thing that binds those who move away from or survive difficult situations is taking action. Doing nothing means that nothing changes.

▶ LEARN Action

Cultivate a Positive Mindset

Here are some questions to challenge your negative self-talk and help you work towards reframing your thoughts to more positive ones; answer them in your notebook.

1. Are you being truly honest with yourself right now? Is the issue that's causing you so much pain as far beyond your control as you think it is, or is there something you can do about it? Write it down. Then write down the solutions you'd offer if you were giving advice to a friend who was in this situation – what would you say?

2. What kind of words are you surrounded by? How do your friends talk? Are they supportive of you? Do they make you feel great? Or are they always criticizing other people and poking fun at anyone who tries and fails? Does this make you afraid to try too? Remember: they're doing this because they're too afraid to try themselves. Do you want to be like them?

3. How do you talk to yourself? What kind of language do you use? Write down five words that you'd use to describe yourself right now. Next, write down five words that you think a good friend would use to describe you. Are they the same as your words? If not, what's the difference? Why do you think that is? Why are you harder on yourself than you would be to someone you care about? Stop being your own Mean Girl.

▲▲▲

Choosing to Think Differently

I was recently asked to interview the participants of the civilian series of *SAS: Who Dares Wins* for the podcast version of the show, and I loved meeting fellow recruits and hearing their stories. I spoke with the winner, James Priestly, an estate agent from Leeds who had an extremely challenging upbringing. He'd been one of the quietest recruits throughout the series – even the SAS men joked that they hadn't even noticed him until the end! He wasn't the fittest, strongest or fastest participant, but he'd quietly and conscientiously just kept going.

I asked James how he'd coped with the torture phase of the show, in which recruits are blindfolded, put into painful stress positions and have to wear headphones playing piercing screams, squealing pigs, crying babies, fingernails running down a blackboard – every kind of horrible noise you can imagine – played on a loop for hours on end.

James smiled and quietly said that he'd 'watched' his favourite film, *Transformers*, in his mind. He'd gone through it frame by frame, from start to finish, noticing every detail. He said he became so distracted by what he was 'watching' that he stopped hearing the horrible noises, stopped feeling the pain in his arms and legs. For him, the hours disappeared because he wasn't focusing on the pain and discomfort of his present situation.

Isn't that incredible? I asked him if he'd ever done anything like that before, or if he'd ever practised meditation or mindfulness. He said he hadn't – he'd just wanted to take himself somewhere else in his head, so that's what he did. I was blown away by this. What James did was impressive, particularly given that he'd never done it before. He'd simply made the decision that that was how he was going to deal with the situation he was in, and he did it. That was how he chose to talk to himself and keep himself going. At that moment, anything that came from *them* disappeared, and it was all about *him* – in the most positive of ways.

This is something that many of us can learn from. It goes back to the problem not always being the problem – it's how we *handle* the problem! Take control of *your* mind, your own happiness. It's *your* responsibility, no one else's. You're in control! We all have decisions to make in life, and while it can seem easier in the short term to wallow in misery and miserable company, you can make the decision to choose to think differently. It really is down to you.

Takeaways to ▶**LEARN**

▶ Sometimes, *you* are the one who's holding you back – so get out of your own way and stop making excuses.

▶ Unless they tell us, we have *no idea* what others are thinking, or why they're behaving the way they are; so we invent stories to suit what we *think* is happening and then make that our truth. So check your facts.

▶ The words we use when we talk to ourselves, and to frame the events around us, have an enormous effect on us; using the right words can shift our perspective from a negative to a positive one.

▶ If there's a problem in our lives right now, rather than dwelling on it, we can think about what we can *learn* from it.

CHAPTER 7

Learning to Fail

You're going to fail way, way more times than you succeed. In fact, that's the very definition of a successful person: someone who just got up and tried again and again and again until they got what they wanted and where they wanted to be. It really is that simple.

Few people have success handed to them on a plate. And if they do, you can bet your life savings they mess it up. Why? Because they haven't learned how to do it properly. All those times you were failing, you were *learning*. They were lessons. It probably didn't feel that way when you were let down, screwed over, embarrassed, broke, scared, lonely, but they were. I'll bet every single time you experienced any of those things you learned something. Even if it was *Well, I won't do that again*, it was a lesson.

British writer Elizabeth Day's book *How To Fail – Everything I've Learned from Things Going Wrong* is a great read on this subject. It's crammed full of enormously successful people talking about what failing has meant to them, what they failed at, and how they brought themselves back from failure. Honestly, it makes you feel so much better about yourself to know that even those who appear to have it all figured out and are smashing it out of the park, have messed up in one way or another. You're not alone! Everybody does it!

It's interesting to note that men and women have wildly differing views on what failure means to them. As you'd expect, men are less forthcoming on the subject, and they are also quick to see the things they're awesome at. Women, and I include myself in this, can show you a list as long as your arm of the things they've got wrong and messed up; however, they struggle to list the things in which they've succeeded.

Failure Is a Matter of Perspective

I'm annoyed with myself that I'm like this. This book is all about making yourself feel amazing, but yup, my go-to place when I think about or describe myself is downwards, not up. I have to *wrench* myself out of this habit. Sometimes I hear myself talking and I think: *How the hell did you end up like this?* I know how: I *used to be* optimistic most of the time, but that was before life had battered me down quite so much. The great thing about life, however, is that despite those times, I still have the power to change, to stop myself in my tracks and choose to think again. And I use it.

Failure also has everything to do with perspective and position. I've been married three times, which is enough to have some of you tittering behind your hands that I clearly like the taste of wedding cake. It's nothing I haven't heard before, so go ahead, get it out of your system! I'm accustomed to being the butt of jokes in the media and at my parents' dinner parties. I used to laugh it off on the outside but die inside at the snide remarks about not taking marriage seriously enough – made by people who knew nothing about the intricacies of my story.

But I don't now. This is just how my life has worked out. I didn't set out for it to be this way. I thought that, just like my parents, I'd marry my teenage sweetheart and stay with them forever; we'd have children, live a comfortable life and retire happy. But that wasn't to be my story, and I'm okay with it.

I subscribe to a podcast by an American businessman called Ed Mylett; I love it because he seems like a caring family man, as well as a driven, compassionate person who's genuinely interested in people's life stories and how they came to find success.

Then one day, while he and an interviewee were talking about marriage, Ed said something along the lines of: 'Why the hell would I take marriage advice from someone who's been married three times?! From someone who clearly doesn't appreciate the institution of marriage and what it represents! Hell, no! I'd take marriage advice from someone who married their first love and stuck with it through hell and high water –that's who I wanna be talking to!'

I remember I was running on the treadmill when I heard Ed make this statement. I'd been a devotee of his podcast because I found it inspiring: just as he'd recommended, I'd started getting up at 5:30 a.m. to go to the gym and push myself through a tough workout before heading for the TV studio, pumped and ready for the day. But this was *me* he was talking about.

By his reasoning, I was a failure. Who the hell was *I* to think I could be any kind of inspiration to anybody? No matter how much good I want to spread to the world, or how much I want to pay it forwards; no matter how thankful I am that I'm in a strong place and can show other women how to believe in themselves, how to stand up for themselves, how to live a great life that they love and to thrive in a way that works for *them* in their own unique way. I was filled with hot embarrassment for even trying, and I felt small and stupid.

I carried on running, not really hearing the rest of that conversation because my head was too busy filling up with negative thoughts and chatter. My chimp brain went into overdrive. Ed was right: I was useless. And then I remembered *why* I'd been married more than once, and *why* those relationships had ended. I remembered how strong I'd been, and how I'd raised my children to be good, kind people. I remembered that I'd never let bitterness enter my heart and had still, despite it all, believed in goodness and love and that was what had brought me Nick.

And I thought: *He's wrong – he's got it all wrong.*

We all have life lessons that we can pass on to our children and others, regardless of how our own lives have worked out.

Perspective is everything: until you've walked in another man or woman's shoes you don't know *why* they made the decisions they did. Learning is acquired through experience, and if your experience is only that of smoothness, joy and light, you'll never understand the strength of character it takes to overcome roughness, sadness and darkness. And if that's the case, what advice do you have to offer?

It's up to us to look for the success in the things we do, especially those that don't turn out the way we'd like them to. I'm not saying that you'll have to get married lots of times before you find happiness. God, no – I hope you don't! But if you do, don't let the opinions of those who don't know you or understand your circumstances make you feel bad about it.

Failure always happens for a reason. You just can't see it at the time. You're too busy hurting and feeling awful to appreciate why something's gone wrong or not worked out. But one thing you have to do is *understand why* something hasn't worked out the way you'd wished, hoped or expected. What can you *learn* from this experience?

An Inevitable Part of Life

Winston Churchill gave good quote and here's one of his finest: 'Success is not final, failure is not fatal. It's the courage to continue that counts.' Isn't that great? I love it because it sums up so neatly what it is we all need to hang onto when things feel like they're going wrong.

It's up there with the phrase 'This too shall pass', which is one I use often to remind myself that even when things are truly awful, it isn't going to last forever. I've been through worse and I will again – this is just one of those times. And when things are good, I remind myself to appreciate them, to savour them, because like a peak in a rollercoaster, there'll always be a dip ahead.

It's important to have a back-up plan for when these challenging moments occur: a go-to bank of solutions that you know work for you. Sadly, this won't include a magic wand to make it all go away – you're going to have to stick it out. Having solutions that help you think clearly makes a huge difference when things go wrong. Because the only thing you can know with any certainty is that *things will go wrong*.

Have a look at this poem[2], which is one of my favourites:

Don't Quit

When things go wrong as they sometimes will,
When the road you're trudging seems all up hill,
When the funds are low and the debts are high
And you want to smile, but you have to sigh,
When care is pressing you down a bit,
Rest if you must, but don't you quit.
Life is strange with its twists and turns
As every one of us sometimes learns
And many a failure comes about
When he might have won had he stuck it out;
Don't give up though the pace seems slow –
You may succeed with another blow.
Success is failure turned inside out –
The silver tint of the clouds of doubt,
And you never can tell just how close you are,
It may be near when it seems so far;
So stick to the fight when you're hardest hit –
It's when things seem worst that you must not quit.

Its author, American Quaker John Greenleaf Whittier, would have been a sure-fire Instagram influencer had he been alive today. Those words were written in the 1800s, but they have as much impact today because as you can see, nothing changes, not really. The failures Whittier spoke of would have been different to those you're facing, but the sentiment is the same: don't give up now, because you just don't know how close you are to succeeding! Imagine how disappointed you'd be if you found out you'd quit just before the point of breakthrough!

There's really only one definition of failure, and that's when we stop trying. Things not working out as you'd planned or wanted, things going wrong, things falling apart, making a mistake, messing up... These are all the same thing, and they're simply a part of life's experience. Some failings will be *huge* – they'll be mortifying, embarrassing on the scale of a YouTube clip gone viral. It doesn't matter. Pick yourself up, dust yourself down, and start all over again. That's it. That's all you can do.

**When failure happens to you –
and it will, probably many, many
times – ask yourself: What am
I meant to learn from this?**

Doing this has been a game changer for me. I can't stress this enough. A. Game. Changer. When things go wrong, once I've got my raging and venting out of the way – yes, I'm a rager and a venter: I need to get all the frustration, anger, hurt and upset out of my system before I can focus on a solution – I look for the lesson. *What am I meant to learn from this?*

Looking for the Lesson

There's always a point to failure, even if it's to teach you never to do something again. That's not failing, that's a life lesson! Once more, it comes down to perspective: it's never the problem that's the problem, it's how you *see* the problem. So, now you've seen it, what are you going to do about it? How do you turn failure into success?

It's not just about being good at something, or even great at it. There are millions of people in the world who never succeed in what they're good and great at. What separates them from the people who *do* succeed is the *determination* to keep trying until they get even better. Not to get complacent when they know they're better than everyone else. To keep practising, training, reaching for more.

In life, there's no one goal to reach and then that's it, we sit around waiting to die. We have to keep going; life is an infinite game that none of us survive! Here's a great quote to illustrate this point: 'We are what we repeatedly do. Excellence, then, is not an act, but a habit.' No, this isn't from some self-help guru or a personal trainer trying to get you to do more push-ups, it was said by a Greek man born in 384BCE: Aristotle, one of the founding fathers of Western philosophy. This is what it reveals: throughout history, humans have experienced adversity, failure and things not working out, and over and over, we've just got up and tried again and again.

The following is an exercise that I do sometimes to remind myself to stay positive when it feels as if everything's going wrong. It may seem negative, but trust me: it works. At one time I didn't tell anyone I did this because I thought it was too strange and dark. Then I saw an Instagram post from bestselling author and blogger Rachel Hollis who was talking about her version of it – and I was so relieved that someone else did it too!

We've all heard about asking ourselves *Will this thing I'm worrying about now matter next year? Or in five years' time? Or at the end of my life?* Chances are that it won't. You can take this a step further, as Pete Cohen suggests in his book *Inspirators: Leading The Way In Leadership*. He asks us to imagine someone reading out our eulogy. What would they say? How would we like to be remembered?

▶ LEARN Action
Live Up to Your Own Eulogy

Imagine your eulogy being read by a loved one at your funeral. It's a weird feeling, but it does make you think. Would they mention your so-called 'failings' or would they talk about everything you tried your best to be? As you consider this, ask yourself the following questions:

1. Is there a difference between what your eulogy would say *now* and what it'd say if you managed to achieve all the things that you're trying to do in life?

2. Where are the gaps? What's being left out?

3. How can you change things so that your life stories match? What do you need to do?

▲ ▲ ▲

Some people take this a stage further and imagine meeting themselves at the gates of heaven. Standing in front of them is the person they had the *potential* to be, had they lived without fear, taken every opportunity that came their way, worked hard and lived a good life. For many of those who do this exercise, their biggest fear is not matching up to the person in front of them. Ed Mylett talks about this often in his podcasts.

Failing My Way to Success

I used to take this exercise a further step and imagine what I would do with my life if I found out I had only a year to live. I dug into it. I felt the horror. But then it became all too real...

Anyone who's had a brush with terminal illness and been fortunate enough to live to tell the tale will know the cold terror that strikes your heart when you're given your diagnosis. No words can truly capture what that moment feels like. I was fortunate in that when I was given mine, the doctor was explaining that I was all clear and I simply needed to 'keep an eye on things'. It was like being run over by a truck and left without a scratch. At the same time I learned I had a potentially fatal disease, I was told the area affected by it had been surgically removed. What does the brain do with this information? It freaks out and runs around in circles.

It turned out that the pain I'd endured for years from endometriosis – which had prompted me to have a full hysterectomy at the age of 46 – had been partly caused by vasculitis, a disease in which the immune system attacks the blood vessels instead of defending them against infection; it can potentially lead to organ failure. I didn't know I had it – no one did – until the tissue removed during my hysterectomy was tested. That led to months of checks on my other organs to see if I had it anywhere else. Thank God that doesn't appear to be the case.

When I found out I had vasculitis my perspective on *everything* changed. I appreciated everything more. I also thought 'fuck it' a lot more and bought myself the convertible sports car I'd always wanted but hadn't because it was impractical. I booked two incredible family holidays and spoiled everyone rotten.

Nick proposed, and after panicking that it would all go wrong because for me marriage means disaster, I said yes. We had a beautiful, quiet wedding with just us and the children and then a fabulous party just for our loved ones. I had a year of doing everything I'd always wanted to do, and I lived life to the full!

I was so busy doing all this that I completely took my eye off the ball with my finances, and clearly went insane. For the first time in my life, I threw caution to the wind, money-wise; I not only stopped saving for a rainy day, I spent my rainy day fund.

I spent every penny I had: all of it. Gone. I spent the money I'd put aside for my tax bill, too, stupidly thinking that because I was well, everything would just magically work out! Life was like a Disney movie!

I told you I went insane. Life isn't like a Disney movie, or a romantic comedy. There's nothing romantic or comedic about completely running out of money! When reality hit me, it was like going from bright sunshine to pitch-black in an instant. What the hell had I done? For the first time in my career, I was faced with calling the Inland Revenue and telling them I didn't have the money to pay my tax bill. It was all my own doing. There was no one else to blame – there had been no global recession, and as yet no coronavirus, and I was still working. I'd just gone mad and spent the lot.

So, I agreed to pay my tax bill in instalments. I took out a loan against my home. I sold my car. I cancelled every membership I couldn't justify – the gym, apps I didn't need, anything. We started using supermarket reward schemes and 'Buy One Get One Free' out of necessity for the first time in a long while. I got a credit card that issued reward points that doubled up and I used it to buy groceries and petrol. I paid off the total amount on the card every month by direct debit and used the points to get things for the house. Christmas was fun, but stripped-back. We didn't take a family holiday for two years.

I felt so unbelievably stupid. Embarrassed. Nick helped me as best he could; by then he was working full-time on the This

Girl Is On Fire website and he took on as much of it as he possibly could to slow the amount of money I needed to pay out. I was the one funding his time and skills, as well as that of the freelancers working for us. I'd put it all in jeopardy by my complete recklessness.

This was why I'd been working flat out after returning from *SAS: Who Dares Wins*. It was why I'd gone into such a tailspin, dealing not only with the box of memories that had been unleashed during my experience there, but also the stress of *needing* to keep working and doing anything I could to keep a roof over our heads and prevent our business from failing before it'd even got off the ground.

The pressure was intense, but it was made more so because I felt as if I'd failed. I'd messed up and it was too embarrassing to admit that to anyone. So I just kept working… until I fell down.

Turning It Around

I've never told anyone this: I was too ashamed. But I see how important it is that you know to what degree I failed and messed up. And how I worked through it. And how, weirdly – I almost want to whisper this because it seems so strange to say it – I'm *grateful* that it happened. When I was in the eye of the storm, it was inconceivable that I'd ever feel gratitude for my situation. But I'm grateful for everything I learned during that time.

I learned *never* to be so stupid again. That's a given. But I also learned how to go back to basics. I'd become comfortable. It'd been years since I'd lived on next to nothing in my London bedsit, putting 50-pence coins into a meter for heat and light, and learning to sit in the dark and cold when I ran out of money. I'd become complacent. Yeah, sure, I deserved to do something nice after my scary diagnosis – I work hard and it's a great feeling to spoil your family – but not like that.

My financial mess meant Nick and I had to look radically at how we ran the This Girl Is On Fire website. I'd been looking at it from a journalistic and philanthropic perspective because that was all I knew. I'm a creative, caring person, so put those two things together and my skillset is in providing a fantastic website full of free, informative, brilliantly written content that helps women feel incredible about themselves.

I'd turned down advertisers and sponsors because I didn't want to dilute the message. I didn't want the site to be filled with those annoying pop-ups you need to keep clicking to get rid of, like an online version of whack-a-mole. I can't stand them. I also didn't want to be associated with any brands that weren't fully aligned with our message. So I turned them all down, even though we really needed the money. We had to find another way to make the site pay for itself – one that kept the brand pure.

We had a long, hard think about what to do. It was really important to me that 90 per cent of the site's content remained free. I strongly believe that feeling great about ourselves is a human right, and as someone who's experienced fear, desperation and low self-worth at the hands of others, I know how important it is to have somewhere to turn that'll freely offer that initial help. I struggled with the idea of charging people anything; surely there had to be another way?

Then I discovered the business advisor and life coach Marie Forleo. She wrote the brilliant book *Everything Is Figureoutable*, which I highly recommend for anyone trying to work out what to do with their life. Reading her story and seeing what a difference she was making to people's lives completely changed my mindset when it came to how the This Girl Is On Fire website should continue.

I saw that I'd been looking at it all wrong. I'd been so blinded by my one mission, which was to help, that I was feeling guilty for making it help *me*. I realized that if I kept doing what I was doing, the site itself would shut down. That meant I wouldn't be helping *anyone*, least of all myself, because I'd made myself sick in the process. The site needed to make enough money to grow bigger and better than anything I could possibly imagine – because the bigger it got, the more women I could help. Making money meant I could pay more people to work on it, which would provide even better content and offer more variety in the tools women had access to.

Also, Nick and I both wanted to link with a charity as soon as we started making money, so we could support women who needed a head start but didn't have the funds to get one. So we decided to form a marketplace. A one-stop shop where women can come and buy products and online services that'll help them improve their lives in every way. We'd already nailed down our three core pillars, but how could we provide services that would help women Live, Learn and Thrive in a Life they Love?

We worked out that our products would be a mixture of life hacks that save time and make life easier, and things that enable women to live a better life, learn new skills to fuel their personal growth and mindset, and also take them to their happy place so they feel the best they can, inside and out.

We put a call-out on our site and that one single video brought a tsunami of replies from businesswomen who had products and services that exactly fitted our criteria. We found that the more meetings we had, the more women were recommended to us. Word of what we were trying to do spread to the point where businesswomen were approaching us, wanting to come on board. It was as if something in the universe switched, and rather than feeling as if I was on my own, pushing and fighting to keep everything going, a thousand hands reached out and supported me.

A Powerful Learning Experience

At that moment, everything changed. Nick came into his own – building relationships with people is what he does best, and he began to thrive, loving the experience of working alongside these incredible women with vision and ambition to match our own. Because of the kind of things we wanted to sell, the women were all of the same mindset: everything they brought to the table would help women feel great and improve their life in some shape or form.

I blossomed because I was able to do what I love: keep the creativity flowing and be the gatekeeper for everything that appears on the site. I surrounded myself with those who are brilliant at what they do – building a business and growing our network – and in doing so I've built a tribe of incredible people who are as committed as I am to making this dream come true.

This Girl Is On Fire is now visited by people in more than 75 countries, and my dream for the site is simple but bold: I want to empower 100 million women around the world to Live, Learn and Thrive in a Life they Love.

I'd never have dared to dream so big if I hadn't failed so spectacularly and had to start all over again.

I'd have carried on, wearing blinkers and not seeing that my good but misguided intentions were limiting me, and us.

One day, there'll be a This Girl Is On Fire presence in every continent on the globe, and all girls and women will be given the education, confidence and skills they need to be capable and self-sufficient. I want every girl, every woman, to feel on fire with self-belief. This is my dream, this is my vision, and one day it'll become a reality.

It feels strange to see this written down: to see gratitude for something that made me feel so wretched, that kept me awake at night with fear and shame. To put it into context, this all coincided with my trying to cope with the memories brought back to life by my *SAS* experience. It all happened at once, so it's no surprise that my brain overloaded!

Hindsight has made me see what a powerful learning experience this time was for me. It's always easier to see clearly when the dust has settled on our problems, which makes that the perfect time to reflect. It's important to look back on times such as the one I've just described, and not simply try to airbrush them out of our mind. Trust me – pushing things to the back of your mind doesn't work! They'll explode out of you at some point in the future.

▶ **LEARN** Action

Review Your Failures

It's well worth taking the time to consider the things in your life that haven't gone the way you'd hoped. Dig out your notebook because I'm going to ask you some questions that may just change the way you look at your life.

1. What have you failed at in life? Write a list of what you think of as your 'failures'. What were the big ones? The smaller ones? Think about personal failures as well as work-related ones: put them all down, get them all out! Leave enough space underneath each one to write notes.

2. What did you learn from those 'failures'? Under each failure in your list, write down the lesson it taught you.

3. Would you have learned those lessons *without* your failures? Be honest in how you answer this! What do you think you would've done if you hadn't experienced those failures? Looking back from where you are now, would you have been happy with that?

4. Would you change anything? Are you glad you went through those experiences because you've learned something about yourself or others? Or do you wish you'd done things differently? If so, what would you change and why? See this as a lesson: you now know how you'd rather react or behave if that situation ever arises again.

▲▲▲

And finally, forgive yourself for failing, for making mistakes. You're not perfect – none of us are. Be thankful that you've had those opportunities to learn and grow. And make sure that's exactly what you do.

Takeaways to ▶LEARN

▶ Failure is simply part of life's experience – *everyone* makes mistakes.

▶ Every failure happens for a reason – and each one offers us a powerful life lesson.

▶ It's worth reflecting on the things in life that haven't worked out in the way we'd hoped: to ask *why* they went wrong and what we *learned* from that experience.

PART III

Thrive

CHAPTER 8

We're All a Mixture of Shit and Brilliance

You know those T-shirts and memes that say 'Be More Beyoncé'? Well, they're all wrong: even Beyoncé herself isn't confident enough to be Beyoncé. When she's shakin' her booty, tossing her incredible head of hair to one side with the wind machine blowing, and looking like a million dollars in gold platforms, she isn't lovely mum-and-wife Beyoncé. No, she's *Sasha Fierce!* Sasha Fierce isn't afraid of any*body* or any*thing*. Sasha Fierce rules the world!

I can't tell you how much better it made me feel when I found out that one of the most successful women on the planet sometimes feels as if she's not good enough. If someone like Beyoncé, who's smart and talented and beautiful, doesn't feel confident enough to jump around on a stage in front of thousands of screaming fans, then maybe it's okay that *I'm* too nervous to get out of my car when I pick up my daughter from dance class because all the mums look at me and I feel that they're not liking what they see.

No One Knows What They're Doing

Everybody has Imposter Syndrome. *Everybody*. Even national leaders get scared that people will find out they don't know what they're doing. It's okay: no one knows what they're doing. Not *all* the time. I mean, yes, of course there are things we know how to do and are very good at, but can we get them absolutely right every single time? No. Most of the time? Probably. Some of the time? Definitely.

People who've trained for years to become experts in their field have to deal with occasions when everything goes wrong; when that happens, they have to fall back on their experience and learning and make stuff up as they go along. Let me be clear, I'm not saying that the world is full of idiots pretending to be heart surgeons. What I mean is that at some point even the best-laid plans go awry and that's when you have to think on the hop, trusting that the outcome will be somewhere close to the original plan.

The people who succeed at this are those who are smart, experienced and can think on their feet. That's completely different to being simply amazing and getting everything right all the time. That never happens. There'll always come a point in your life, whether at work or in your personal life, when you're winging it. And then it could all go brilliantly or it could all go very badly.

My husband summed this up so well a couple of years ago after we'd left a meeting with a very successful television company in London. We'd pitched a TV idea to them, hoping they'd help us get it to a bigger market. They'd liked it and after many months of negotiating and to-ing and fro-ing we'd not only signed a deal with them, but were also on the verge of signing a massive deal with a huge US network.

It was a big thing for us because it meant people would finally take our little company seriously – we had so many more ideas that we wanted to get out there! Nick doesn't have a television background, but he's one of the most creative, funny and driven men I know and has brilliant ideas bubbling up all the time.

As we were walking down the street after our meeting Nick said, 'You know, I'm just as good as them at working on ideas.' I nodded in agreement and he continued, 'I can be just as shit and just as good as them.'

He looked taken aback, as if he'd made the biggest discovery. You see, because he doesn't come from the TV world and started dreaming up ideas relatively late in life (in his mid-40s), he'd always felt he wasn't taken seriously in meetings. To be fair to him, neither of us was taken seriously in meetings – I was just more used to it than him.

Trust me, not being taken seriously is something I've been up against every step of my career. I've either been too young, too nice (yes, really), too similar to someone else, too Daytime TV, and now as I enter my 50s, too old. How's that for luck? People outside of the TV world think it's glamorous and easy and fun, which of course it can be, but it's also BRUTAL. It can be quite snooty to outsiders, too – 'civilians' who dare to think that they can waltz in and work in telly 'just like that' – and Nick had felt it.

But after many meetings with the company we'd signed a deal with, ironing out the kinks in the show to smooth negotiations with the US network, Nick realized that whilst he didn't have TV industry experience, he sure as hell knew how to work on a good idea and how to do business. And, importantly, he knew he could be just as shit and just as good as the people he was working with.

You see we tend to judge ourselves by other people's highlights reel while looking at our own blooper tape.

We don't see other people's mistakes, hear their worries, feel their fears – we just think they know what they're doing and we don't.

But the truth is: we're *all* a mixture of shit and brilliance. This is *so* important to understand. In fact, it's so important that I'll say it again: *no one knows what they're doing.*

Just Winging It

I didn't realize this until recently, when I branched out into the corporate world, away from the slightly insane TV world. In TV land, everybody says that things are marvellous, even when it's as plain as the nose on your face that they're anything but. They'll tell you that you're 'wonderful, darling!' one day and fire you the next. *Everything* is a great idea if *they* thought of it – it only becomes a bad idea when it absolutely doesn't work, and then it mysteriously becomes *someone else's bad idea*.

I thought it was only in TV that this happened, until I started a business and had to talk to people in the 'real world'. Then I realized that *everyone* is faking it. Some people clearly have a good idea about what they *should* be doing, but have no clue as to how to *actually* do it. So they just kind of muddle along until it all works out. I didn't know this. Because I've always worked in the creative world, I thought that anyone who wears a suit, male or female, is *very clever* and should be listened to. A maths teacher for instance, or someone like that. Then I realized that everyone's winging it.

For me, this was a game changer. I stopped being scared of people in suits. I realized that while I'm good at *my* job – which involves words and making people feel comfortable talking about themselves – and they're good at *theirs* – which involves spreadsheets and saying 'no' a lot – it doesn't mean they're smarter than me. It just means that we're good at different things.

The whole world is winging it, so that means you've just as much chance of succeeding as anyone else. You just have to believe in yourself, learn about what you want to do, make a plan and then try damn hard to make it happen. And if the first plan doesn't work, make another plan.

That's the easy part. The hard part is keeping going, because I can guarantee it's not going to work the first time. And possibly not the second time, either. Or the third. If it does, then you'll have been *very lucky*. But you'll still need to keep an eye on things because it won't work that way forever. However, you *will* be able to handle it, even when it doesn't feel as if you can. Because you're winging it, just like everyone else.

Mel C from the Spice Girls put it this way in an interview with *Women's Health* magazine: 'We all have these feelings, nobody's got this shit together. We're all over the place. We have good days and we have bad days. You're not weird and you're not on your own.' I saw this quote on the group's Instagram page and saved it because it instantly made me feel better about myself. If someone as supremely talented and successful as Mel C feels that she doesn't always know what she's doing, then it's okay for us mere mortals to feel the same!

The thing is, we all have a unique skillset and we're all different. We work at our individual levels, at our own pace; we have our own things that we find easy and interesting compared to everyone else. And thank God for that because otherwise the world would only have accountants or tree surgeons. Thank

God we're so different; that's how we all slot in and can work together.

Some people hold to the theory that only the most meticulously prepared people can afford to wing it because they're doing so within the parameters of *actually knowing* what they're doing. I don't call that winging it: I call that 'normal working'. That's being responsible and prepared for any eventuality; it's being fluid enough to go with the flow when things change. As they always do.

Truly winging it is turning up for work having no idea that you're supposed to be doing a presentation, scrabbling one together and managing to do an okay job of it. That works once in a while, but at some point you'll land flat on your face because you're taking the piss.

Pushing Ourselves Out There

Being a true mixture of shit and brilliance is loving what you do to the point where you keep trying new things and push your own boundaries. You learn as much as you can about the level you're at and scare yourself a little by trying something different. You'll probably mess it up. But you'll learn something from that, and you can use it the next time you try it.

Sometimes you'll be brilliant – you'll absolutely storm it and all those lessons will come together. Purely winging it, day in day out, shows only that you don't really care about what you're doing. That you don't have any goals or outcomes for what you're doing – instead you're just, well, doing it. This means you're busy but not productive, and there's a big difference between those things. If you truly want to be in charge of your own destiny, you have to know what it is that you're aiming for, what your goal is. Because how will you know if you've reached it otherwise?

Learn as much as you can about what you're working on, or want to work on – even if that means working on yourself rather than a 'project'. Getting as much information and experience as you can is invaluable, and it doesn't have to cost you anything. Rachel Hollis, the hugely successful author of *Girl Wash Your Face* and an inspiring force of support for millions of women around the world, has made a whole career based on the fact that she got where she is with a high-school diploma and a Google search bar.

There are YouTube tutorials for anything and everything, podcasts by experts in their field, films to watch and learn from – the world literally is in your hands when it comes to knowledge and inspiration. So don't let 'not knowing' be the reason you're holding yourself back. Seek out someone who's doing what you want to do and watch what they do, how they do it, and follow them.

We all bring a unique spin to whatever we try; we have our own voice, and there's never been a better time to use yours.

Watch, look, listen, learn... It's all out there. Once you have a plan, once you have goals and have taken the steps towards absorbing and learning as much as you possibly can about your chosen field, put yourself out there and don't be afraid of being a mixture of shit and brilliance. Your reward will be a sense of happiness, fulfilment and satisfaction that comes from trying your best.

Isn't happiness all we hope for anyway? Isn't this what life's supposed to be all about? If you could find a formula for happiness, you'd be a gazillionaire. Happiness is the one emotion that we're all equal in longing for and it's the one that has complete disregard for who or what we are.

Now, I've read many a millionaire's claim that they've been happy and rich and happy and poor, and happy and rich is much better. I understand that: money worries are a key cause of stress and relationship breakdown all around the world. Not having enough money to live on *sucks*. But *having* money doesn't automatically make you happy, and I think this is one of the biggest misconceptions we have about life.

Do you remember that old song by Crowded House called 'Weather With You'? It was one of my favourites. Basically, what it's saying is that it doesn't matter where you are, because wherever you go you take the weather with you. So if you're pissed off at life in general, winning the lottery may get you a snazzier car and a bigger house, but I guarantee that in no time at all you'll be pissed off again.

Balancing Brilliant and Bad

You see, it's not just *us* that's a mixture of shit and brilliance: it's *life itself*. Just as you'll never be purely brilliant at everything you do, life will also have days that are less than perfect. So, how do you find the balance between the two?

Step 1: You stop doing what makes you feel shit.

Step 2: You do what makes you feel brilliant.

Obviously, nothing in life is that simple. Even doing things that are brilliant can get annoying after a while, and we'll want to do something else. We humans are very strange and we like to keep ourselves on our toes. When we finally find something that absolutely floats our boat and is our favourite thing of *all time*, once we've done it for a while something clicks in our head and we get bored of it.

If we could spend the rest of our lives eating just ice cream, or cake or hamburgers – or whatever – it would be fantastic for, I don't know, two days, a week, a month... Then we'd get very, very bored with just cake and hamburgers. They just wouldn't seem as great any more. Which is a real shame because you love cake and hamburgers, right?

It's the same with doing brilliant things. If you're willing to chase a dream, it means that you're going to be thinking about it and working on it 24/7 for a very long time. So you'd better be pretty damn sure that you like it. Sure that it makes you feel excited every time you think about it; that you can't imagine life without it; that you feel good when you imagine what it'll feel like once you've achieved it. And then what you'll do *afterwards*.

It's a lot like being in love. Falling in love is wonderful. Oh my God, the rush! The churning stomach! The incessant thoughts! The sex! And then, well, you know: you move in together and you realize it's not all champagne and oysters (or whatever floats your romantic boat) – it's pasta and laundry.

But you still love each other, right? You still want to work at it. You still get that flutter, of course you do, just not *every* moment of *every* day. But you can't imagine your life without the other person, and when it comes down to it, you'd be crushed if it all fell apart or if anyone else decided they wanted what you have and tried to take it from you… *That's* what working on your dream of having a brilliant life is like.

▶ THRIVE Action

Create a Brilliant, Balanced Life

The key here is to be grateful for what you *have*, while working towards what you *want*. Have a think about this and then grab your notebook and jot down your response to these questions:

1. Which things in your life do you think are brilliant?

2. What's going really well for you?

3. What's *not* going so well?

4. What things could you improve?

5. What would you like to be better in your life, or what would you like to be better at?

▲▲▲

Finding and Doing Work We Love

So, what do you love doing and are brilliant at, and how can you make money out of it? Does that seem terribly un-British and crass? To want to make money out of something you *like?* Aren't we supposed to just go to school, then take off that uniform and swap it for an office uniform, then take that off and swap it for our retired uniform and then *die?* You'd think so, the way we behave.

Where's the joy in that? In fact, when was the last time you thought about what gives you *joy* in life? If that doesn't work for you right now, flip it on its head: what's happening now that's making you feel so bad that you'd do *anything* to get away from it?

Have a think about it: is there a connection between the things that are brilliant and the things that are shit? Are they at opposite ends of the same scale? Is there something you can do to change that? For example, are you brilliant at something but it's not paying you enough money to cover your rent? Is there a way of utilizing your skill in a way that fulfils other people's needs, so that they can pay you? That way you'll be doing something that you enjoy, that you're brilliant at, *and* the pay will be amazing.

Contrary to what you may have had drummed into you, all work doesn't have to involve blood, sweat and tears. You're *allowed* to enjoy your work *and* be well rewarded for it. It's not just bad guys and city slickers who make good money; there's no direct correlation between being poor and good and rich and bad – despite what every fairy tale and Hollywood blockbuster tells you. It's okay. In fact, I'd say it should be the goal of *every one of us* to do something we love and get paid well for it. Wouldn't you?

▶ THRIVE Action
Identify Your Brilliant Job

1. Write a list of the things that make you feel brilliant, that light a fire inside you. Be honest, even if they're embarrassing. They can be anything.

2. Now think of *situations* that would make you feel those emotions.

3. Next, think of *jobs* that involve those situations, those emotions, and let them sit with you for a while. Have you ever thought about doing them? Why not? Who says you can't?

▲▲▲

My Shit-to-Brilliant Career Path

As I mentioned earlier, after I left college, I worked for six months in an office. It was a truly awful environment, rife with sexism and intimidation. I put up with it because I kept hoping it'd get better. It didn't. It sucked. This was the early 1990s and sexism was so widespread it simply registered as something dreadful that everyone had to put up with. And I just wanted to get on with doing my job.

Eventually, I quit after my boss humiliated me in front of a male co-worker, just for kicks. At the end of one day he asked me to stay behind to do some filing. He then sat watching, with his feet up on his desk and his hands behind his head, as I shifted heavy files from one part of the office to another and loaded them onto shelves, stretching up high and bending over low in front of him as I did so. And when he 'changed his mind' I had to move them all back again.

The other man was horrified and I heard him mutter, 'Why the hell are you doing that?'

'Because I can...' came the smirking reply.

The next day I went to see my boss's boss, our head of department, to ask why my male colleague, who was only 18 and less qualified than me, was being taken out to lunch to meet clients whereas I had to stay behind and do the filing. Interesting side note here: I hadn't gone to complain about my boss's sexist behaviour – instead, I'd kept it to 'business' so that hopefully I'd be able to get out of the office more often, feel more stimulated in my work and not have to deal with my boss on a daily basis.

The head of department exploded with rage – I'd never seen someone so affronted. I should be grateful to have the job, he told me. Who the hell did I think I was? In his country (he wasn't from the UK) it took seven years for a woman to be allowed to meet clients, *and* they'd be made to walk out the door *backwards* as a mark of respect. He was furious. I left the room, quietly returned to my desk and started planning my letter of resignation.

I went into work the following day with a resignation letter addressed to the head of HR and the head of our department; I also posted a copy to the CEO of the company, who was based overseas. I've always kept a personal journal and that habit of writing about my day meant I had a detailed account of every terrible thing my boss had said and done. Other women in the company had told me they'd been through the same thing, but when they'd spoken up they'd been moved into other departments and told to keep quiet. Nothing had been done.

It felt so wrong that that man was still there, feet up on his desk, smirking. So I told as many people as I could higher up the chain about what he and the company were like, then quit and left him behind. Many years later I heard from someone who worked for the company that my old boss was still there. Nothing. Had. Changed.

But I'd changed. I'd taken steps to move away from a bad situation towards a brilliant one. I'd wanted to be free of my boss, to work creatively, to do exciting things that stimulated me. None of those things were ever going to happen in that company, and with hindsight, quitting changed my life in every conceivable way.

I went backpacking around the world, I met wonderful people, I had adventures, and I carried on with that habit of writing detailed journals about what was happening to me. They formed the basis of articles that I had published when I returned to the UK. That helped me get into journalism college, which helped me get a job in London, which led me to where I am today.

I've always worked hard, and I've been incredibly lucky to be in an industry that has allowed me to do some really cool and exciting things. I've genuinely loved most of my working life because of the interesting people I've met and the fun things I've got to do. I've had jobs that paid well and jobs that paid terribly, but I've taken them all because they're interesting and I've enjoyed them.

But as always, there's shit mixed in with the brilliance. My job is incredibly insecure; I never know from one year to the next if I'm going to be rehired. Sometimes from one month to the next! That's quite a nerve jangler when you're the breadwinner and a single parent. Everything I do is scrutinized and flipped inside out and turned into ridiculous cover stories for trashy magazines – the truth rarely gets in the way of a good headline.

The people in my life who I properly know and love realize that it comes with the territory and have stopped getting upset over every headline.

I'll give you an example of this: an absolute corker. I was once pictured on the front cover of a magazine with a very worried expression and a headline screaming: 'Andrea's night of shame!' I gulped when I heard about that one – what had I done?! The truth was… One night while slaving over a hot laptop writing my column I ate a whole tub of chocolate rice krispie cakes – well, they *were* delicious! – and put out a jokey tweet saying something like, 'Oh, the shame of it!' The photo was one that a paparazzo had taken while I was distractedly looking for my car. You know, that 'Where the hell did I park it this time?' look. That was it – the shameful story.

And today my daughter told me that her friend had told her that her mum had told her that a magazine had said I'm pregnant. Seeing as I don't have a womb that would quite literally be a miracle. Nope, I'm not pregnant – I just need to work on those abs a little more.

The Grit that Creates the Pearl

So, with everything we do in life, there'll always be a mixture of shit and brilliance. Sometimes everything will go amazingly – you'll read this book, get fired up with confidence and truly believe that you can do all the things you ever wished you could.

By the way, can I say right now that YES, YOU'RE AMAZING, and YES, YOU CAN DO IT! That's the brilliant bit.

The other bit (some may say it's the shit part, but I'd say it's just life) is that you have to do it yourself – no one is going to do 'it' for you. I like to think of that bit as the grit that makes the pearl. A pearl is formed as a result of a tiny bit of grit that gets inside an oyster shell and agitates it. In order to stop it rubbing, the oyster surrounds the grit in a substance that, over time, becomes a pearl – one of nature's most special offerings.

Each pearl is a thing of unique beauty and no two are alike. We too are unique and we experience our own unique difficulties, our own grit, which will eventually, once we learn the lesson it's trying to teach us, become a thing of beauty.

Letting go of the idea of perfection – of 'life will be better when…' – is the biggest lesson we can learn. Perfection doesn't exist! There'll always be people able to do things better than you, who are more experienced than you, who are further down the road than you. But they'll also mess things up, just as you do.

Your potential for brilliance is the same as for any man or woman, but it's important to find it in something that makes you happy.

Surely being brilliant at *that* is the one thing we should *all* be striving for? My advice to you is to accept that nothing in life is as perfect as it looks on the outside – *everything* has that one piece of grit that makes life uncomfortable.

So, what's the grit that's making your pearl – and how can you make it work for you? Here's an example: you hate your job and all you can think of is leaving it, walking away. However, there are no other jobs out there and so you're trapped. Can you think of a way to make the job you're doing work better for you? Perhaps you can ask for more training, covered by the company, so you'll add to your skillset and make yourself more employable?

That small action will help you feel less hopeless about where you are – because you'll have taken a positive, helpful step to move forwards. You may even end up with a promotion because you've become more skilled, and that will take you away from the job you hated in the first place!

Don't fret if things don't work out right away, or if you feel as if other people are better than you or way ahead of you. We're all on our own paths, and we all have our strengths and weaknesses. Find your brilliance, work at it, hone it and then let it shine.

Takeaways to ▶**THRIVE**

▶ At some point, we all have to wing it, and whether we're winging it at work or in our personal life, it could all go brilliantly or it could all go to shit. That's just life.

▶ To take charge of our own destiny, we need to know what we're aiming for: if we don't know our goal, how will we know when we've reached it?

▶ Nothing in life is as perfect as it looks on the outside: we all have a piece of grit that makes life uncomfortable – but that grit can make a pearl.

CHAPTER 9

How to Know When Your Dreams Have Come True

As I explained earlier, when I was younger, it didn't occur to me that I *couldn't* do something. So I just went for it, fully expecting that everything would work out okay. I wanted to be a journalist in London, so I did it! Okay, it wasn't quite as straightforward as that: what happened was I moved to London, slept on people's floors, moved into a scary bedsit the size of a disabled toilet as it was all I could afford, got a student loan, went to college, worked for free for anyone who'd have me, kept writing and submitting articles to anyone who'd accept them and many who didn't, and applied for every job going.

And then, ooh, just like that, I became a proper, paid staff journalist! The job wasn't at the magazine I'd wanted to work for, and it didn't pay what I needed, never mind wanted, but I was doing what I'd set out to do. So technically, my dream had come true.

There are two lessons to be learned here:

1. Your dream will come true if you believe in yourself, work very hard and put yourself out there to fail.

2. Your dream that has come true won't look the way you imagined it. It won't be exactly the same. In fact, sometimes, you'll have to look around you before you realize, *Oh my God, this is it – it's actually happened!* Because life isn't like in the movies, where music plays and the sun sets and everything's wonderful. This is real life, and it won't all be perfect. Remember that.

The Power of Visualization

Many schools of thought hold that we should be really specific about what it is we're dreaming of. That we should write down our dreams every day, as if they've already happened, and see and feel our success as if we're already living it. I can see the logic in that, and it has really helped me in terms of nailing down where I see myself in the future – where my 'future self' will be living, how she'll feel, dress, think, do, etc.

Visualizing our dreams in this way puts us into a state whereby everything we do to move towards our success feels natural and less frightening because the brain has already thought it through. It knows it'll all be okay so it doesn't freak out with all the usual *Yeah, but what if...* scenarios that ruin all the best-laid plans.

Fear holds us back way more than lack of skill or opportunity. This is why it's not always the people who are the best at things who make it – it's the people who've believed in themselves and what they're doing and who've seen themselves, over and over again, reaching their goal. Every step they take that brings them closer towards it feels natural, as if it was meant to be. The brain doesn't step in with its fight or flight response to challenge their success because it already knows the outcome – they're going to make it.

It's not just wishful thinking either: this process of visualizing our future working out in the way we want it to has been scientifically proven to help us achieve our goals. Every athlete who has achieved major success has used this technique: repeatedly visualizing the race, the match, the game, whatever it is they're competing in. They imagine themselves getting ready, what they'll wear, how they'll stand, what they'll be doing when the whistle blows, how they'll pace themselves, when they'll exert themselves. Golfers visualize the course – picturing every hole and where they want the ball to land, which club they'll use, and how they're going to sink that putt.

They do this over and over again until it becomes natural. And when the big day comes, their performance nerves are massively reduced because everything they do feels familiar. We all know that we perform better when we're relaxed and familiar with our surroundings and the people around us – it helps reduce our fear and anxiety so we can just get on with whatever it is we have to be getting on with.

Now this doesn't come easily, or even naturally, because our basic instinct is to feel fear, especially when we're pushing ourselves beyond our comfort zone. And we all know that growth of any kind has to happen outside of our comfort zone; comfort is where we sit, outside of it is where we run.

No Such Thing as Overnight Success

I visualize my goals, but I still have times when it all seems pointless and futile, especially when things seem to be going backwards rather than forwards. How many times have we dreamed, made detailed plans, put them out to the universe, taken all the big steps we needed to take, worked hard, put in the hours, only to be standing one year later in exactly the same position, if not worse? It's pretty hard to live off dreams, plans and optimism when nothing is working out – optimism doesn't pay the bills.

The key word missing here is *yet*. It's not working out *yet*. The thing to remember about success is that it doesn't come with a big bang. It's important to look at success in exactly the same way that we look at failure. We know that failure doesn't happen overnight – it's a build-up of tiny little things going wrong over a prolonged period of time until one day it hits tipping point and that's it! It's done!

Anyone who's been in a relationship that hasn't worked out, a job they hated, even having a body they don't recognize, knows that none of these things happen in an instant. One forgotten birthday card didn't mark the death knell of a romance. One under-prepared meeting didn't mean the end of a job. One bar of chocolate didn't add that extra 10 pounds. It all happened gradually, over time, bit by bit.

One day you realize you're overweight, unemployed and single – and you can bet that didn't happen overnight. While you're doing them, you don't even notice those little negative, self-sabotaging things that gradually become your normal. These things take time.

Right now, you're exactly where you should be on your journey to success, failure or even stagnation – it depends on everything you've been doing to get to here. It's been within your control all along – it's just that sometimes you can't see it. Sometimes you don't *want* to see it because it's *far* easier to blame everyone and everything else for stuff that hasn't gone your way. Good intentions mean nothing if they're lying by the wayside. You need to do it to get it.

Setting the Destination

So, how do you know whether things are falling together rather than falling apart? First things first: be really honest with yourself. Have you thought about where you want to be, or are you just aimlessly drifting, wishing things were better but not really sure how? If that's you – wake up! How will you know you've succeeded if you don't even know what success looks like to you?

It's like getting into a car and knowing you want to be some place but you aren't sure where. How the hell do you know when you've arrived if you don't know your destination? You'll be driving around for the rest of your life, literally getting nowhere, until you give up, pull over and decide 'this will do'; or you'll run out of petrol and blame everyone else for it. Neither is a good option. So don't do that.

Have you had dreams and made plans and done absolutely *nothing* about them? Be honest now. How many times have you said something like, 'Yeah, *this* is the year I'm going to get really fit, like JLo' – and then not done a single thing towards it? No surprises for guessing the outcome of that approach. JLo doesn't look like a smokin' hot mama through luck – although, sure, there are some handy genes at play. She also works out, eats clean, and sleeps for 10 hours a night. (To be honest, I'm as impressed with the sleep as I am with her incredible body.)

Making any kind of positive change starts with you. And you need to keep going, even if it feels like you're getting nowhere. Especially then.

It's hard, and it seems utterly pointless and disheartening. Everyone else seems to be streaking past you to the finish line. But that's when you have to remember this isn't a normal race where we're all heading to the same finish line. There will be many finish lines because once you hit one, you'll set yourself another goal and will start heading for that one, and then another and another! That's why a lot of the time we barely notice our success – because we keep moving the damn finish line.

Seeing and Feeling My Dream

I've experienced this for myself. Nick and I had been developing the This Girl Is On Fire site for just over a year, and we were working hard, putting out amazing content and getting great feedback from our community about how much it was helping them. That made me feel good, but I was too exhausted by the running of it, of doing a hundred other jobs to pay for it, to really take in the compliments. The site had become a monster that needed feeding.

I suddenly realized that the only person *not* getting anything from the site was *me*: the person who'd started it! Nick was loving designing it and putting it together; our content editor Jayne was loving getting all the freelance features in and commissioning amazing pieces that were helping women live better lives; our social media editor Emma was loving being able to work for a company that allows her to express herself creatively alongside running a busy house with three young children.

They were all having a great time, but I was exhausted and resentful. By all accounts, the website, my dream, was a runaway success. It was doing exactly what I wanted it to do; the feedback we were getting was incredible and so many people wanted to come on board with us and were giving us their support. The universe was on our side!

But the universe wasn't paying the bills – I was. The site had started organically – purely from a place of wanting to help women feel great about themselves and get the life they deserve – so I hadn't thought through what I'd do when it started taking off. I hadn't considered it would take more people to run it; that they'd all need to be paid and it was me who'd have to find the funds. I was so focused on the site being amazing, the content being free and accessible and everyone enjoying working there, that I'd forgotten about myself. Its very success nearly broke me. I burned out.

It may seem strange to include my burnout in a chapter about success, but bear with me. Collapsing at work may not seem like a sign of success, but what that moment did was force me to stop and recalibrate my thinking. I dealt with the issues in my personal life that had been building up inside me like a pressure cooker ready to explode – I got help. I stopped and re-thought *everything* about the site.

And I stopped pushing. I stepped back. I looked at things from the outside and realized what I'd been doing. I'd been so 'in it' that I hadn't seen clearly that whilst my intentions were good, my execution was poorly conceived. I was exactly where I should have been because of everything I'd been doing. In other words, the site was doing everything I wanted it to do and I was falling apart because I'd placed the burden of keeping it going squarely on my own shoulders.

Being on the brink of burnout didn't happen overnight; it happened because of a thousand things that I'd done beforehand and was continuing to do. I simply hadn't known any better, so my mistakes had gone unnoticed. And I'd kept on making them.

So I started looking at things differently. Rather than flailing around, raging and resentful at everything that was making me exhausted and all the difficulties I was facing, I made a conscious effort *not* to look at everything from a place of lack.

It was like scales falling from my eyes. I looked at all the things I had rather than the things I didn't. I *really* saw them, felt them and was grateful for them. And then I realized that everything I had was what I'd been wishing for. The problems, the post-traumatic stress from my past, the anger I felt with myself for getting us into financial difficulties – all of these were still there, *but so were the successes*. And once I realized they'd been creeping in, and that I just hadn't taken the time to see and enjoy and appreciate them, I saw that just as death can come by a thousand cuts, so too can success.

**Mistakes don't mean you're failing – as long
as your momentum is carrying you forwards,
towards your goals, you're still succeeding.**

You just need to stop and check that what you're doing and how you're doing it is happening in a way that works for you. If it's not, you've not failed, you've *learned*. Learn your lesson, make the changes, and carry on. You're always where you're supposed to be, and things are happening in the order they're supposed to – not in the order *you* necessarily wanted them to. You *are* getting there.

Thanking Our Obstacles

Stop. Think. Look around. What things do you have now that you'd wished for earlier in your life? When you achieved them, did you take the time to enjoy them and savour them, or did you just tick the list and move on to the next thing without feeling the joy of achievement? You'll *never* be happy if you don't take that time, and I know this first-hand. Nick admitted to me that he used to do this – he'd dream and save and finally get the one thing he'd been aiming for, only to use it a couple of times and then start planning for the next shiny object that he thought would make him happy, make him a success.

Stop that. In fact, just stop.

Cinderella called a dream 'a wish your heart makes', so take the time to see and feel when your dreams have come true, even if they don't look exactly how you thought they would. You'll feel it in your heart as much as your head because that's where all dreams begin.

The next thing to do on your journey to appreciating your successes is to thank your obstacles. A friend of mine did this recently and it was a *game changer*. She was having a really difficult time at work with a woman who was gunning for her job. It was tough, really tough, because previously she'd liked and trusted this person. She took it really personally and was understandably upset, hurt and angry.

It was all really unfair, she said. Why wasn't her boss doing anything about it? Were they trying to get rid of her? Was everyone in on it?! She started noticing slights, confrontation, atmosphere and attitude. Before long, she felt sick at the thought of going into work, and was on guard for the woman and the other colleagues involved; her antennae were up, looking for glances, comments, hurtful asides. Not surprisingly, she found them – it's funny how if that's what we're looking for, they sure as hell will turn up.

Then my friend realized she couldn't just sit around wallowing. She had bills to pay and needed her job, so she had to fight back, even if she never actually confronted this woman and the colleagues who now seemed to be sneakily siding with her. So she dug in and got better at her job. She researched more than everyone else before meetings, took more interest, became more focused, dressed better, got in early, and was engaged and energized rather than depressed and feeling like a victim. It was *hard* and in the beginning she was faking it until she felt it. And she *really* didn't feel it.

Then one day she noticed that the other woman had backed off a little and wasn't being quite so aggressive – both passively and otherwise. Others were listening more to my friend in meetings. She realized then that she owed this woman a huge thank you: because she'd made her raise her game. She'd fallen out of love with her job and had felt overlooked and undervalued, so she'd given up. Her energy had been low and she'd given off negative vibes. In fact, she admitted she'd been coasting. It was no wonder the other woman was gunning for her job – she quite rightly thought she could do it better!

My friend stopped feeling victimized and as if the whole thing was unfair. She changed her mindset. Today, she's not the best of buddies with this other woman, but she can see that she and the team look at her differently and that she's re-earned their respect. She's grateful now that her adversary hadn't done what she'd wanted her to do – be kind to her while she was feeling low and nurture her – because that would have kept her where she was, making all the same mistakes.

By competing for her role, this colleague actually forced my friend to dig deep, rise up, and remember why she loved her job so much. Because she'd been an utter bitch, she'd made my friend better at her job. So now, rather than feeling a knot in her stomach whenever she sees the woman, my friend silently thanks her for everything she's given her. She turned what was a problematic situation into a success. She gave my friend her dream job and it was the one she'd had all along but had just lost sight of.

So, the lesson to be learned here is to thank your obstacles! What have you had to learn in life? How have you overcome it? Is it an opportunity to improve?

In terms of being liked at work, I get it – I'd feel exactly the same. I like being liked: it's my kryptonite. I know it has held me back in every single part of my life: I've squirmed and wriggled like a dog on her back, licking her chops nervously and weakly wagging her tail in the hope that people will be kind. I'm embarrassed when I think back on that now. No wonder they were so disdainful: I was pitiful! It's made me weak.

Who doesn't like being liked – it's awesome and it makes you feel amazing! But if someone *doesn't* like you, particularly if you have to work with them day in day out, it's best to accept now that although it's a shame, it just isn't meant to be. Keep the relationship a respectful, professional one.

I've realized that being liked isn't the same as being respected, and I know which one I'd rather have – respect. Respect for myself and for others keeps me grounded and kind, as well as loyal and supportive to people around me. Remember: people can like you for all kinds of reasons, and not all of them are good for you. They may like you because you always do what they want, you don't fight back, and you bend over backwards to keep the peace. That kind of 'like' only works because it suits them: it has no respect at its core.

I realize now that, for a while, I lost the self-respect that I instinctively had when I was younger, my ability to stay true to myself. Back then I didn't care what the school bullies thought of me when I was doing my own thing because I wasn't hoping that one day they'd 'like' me. It's good to have that self-respect back again.

Seeing the Dream Through

In order for your dreams to come true you need to have enough self-respect to finish what you started. This is something that we're all guilty of: I have notebooks filled with crazy, ambitious ideas that have never seen the light of day, and I bet you do too.

Do you know the real reason you come up with *amazing ideas* about a company you're going to start, a job you're going to go for, a book you're going to write, a course you're going to attend, and then you just... well... *don't?* Do you procrastinate? Do you start jobs and never finish them? Are you entertaining and wonderful company at the start of a friendship and then slowly drift away once that person becomes too close? I didn't even realize I did this until recently, and I was horrified.

Why do we do this to ourselves? Why on earth would we jeopardize our own success and stop our dreams in their tracks? Here's why:

In our own unique way, we sabotage our dreams because we're afraid we're going to be judged.

We turn up at the start of a new relationship – and that includes friendships – all shiny and witty and engaged and much more fun than we really are. We make people fall in love with us and when they do, and we realize that they're going to stay around, it becomes too hard to keep that awesomeness going. So we drift away.

I thought it was other people who drifted away from me – I genuinely never realized it was me who drifted away from them. I did this because I was scared they would find out that I'm not as great as they thought I was; I drifted away before they figured it out. Which is a pretty stupid thing to do because if we keep doing it we'll end up with no friends and feeling pretty rubbish about ourselves.

When it comes to all those amazing hobbies and work things, you stop doing them because a) it's easy to start but really, really hard to keep going, and b) if you keep going then you'll have to finish. And what if you do it and everyone thinks it's terrible and you wish you'd never done it? It's way easier to say it didn't work out, that you gave it a go but it was turned down, or the guy moved away, or someone never returned your call – whatever excuse makes you feel better.

And you know what's funny? No one will care because everyone does exactly the same thing. Actually, *your* not finishing something makes them feel better about themselves, and everyone can carry on with their life without feeling inadequate because of your awesomeness.

The biggest obstacle you'll have to face when it comes to achieving your dreams isn't people thinking they're stupid and ridiculing you for them – it's them hating you because you've dared to succeed where *they* have failed. Your success holds a mirror up to every time they gave up, and they'll not thank you for it.

But – and remember this before you think there's no point in even trying – those who *really love you* will applaud you. Those above you will celebrate you. Those beneath you would never have supported you anyway, and it'll be devastating when you discover who those people are. But you have to move on.

Don't be so afraid of your light that you hide in the dark. No dream ever came true by being dimmed and put to one side because you're afraid of what other people will think of it.

**Dreams come true because they're put into
sunlight and fed and watered and loved
until they grow into something beautiful.**

Your dreams may not appear in exactly the way you'd planned, but they'll be beautiful nonetheless. Are you deliberately stopping yourself from achieving success because you're worried about what other people might think about you? If you keep changing your *definition* of success, ultimately you'll *never* achieve it. Is this something that you do?

▶ THRIVE Action

Revive Your Dreams

Think about the things that you've aimed for over the years – at some point in your life you'll have had an idea about where you want to be and what you want to be doing. Write them down and then ask yourself these questions:

~ Are you close to doing or being those things? Or are you still way off track?

~ If you've already achieved those things, have you been so busy pushing forwards that you've not taken the time to appreciate that the life you're living now is the one you once dreamed of having?

▲ ▲ ▲

Think back to the earlier *Action* about imagining your eulogy. Do you want to be remembered as someone who never tried because they were afraid of failing? Or half tried for the same reason? Or was so busy pushing that they never stopped to appreciate how far they'd come? These scenarios may come from opposite ends of the spectrum, but the results are the same: you'll never see success. Either because you'll never achieve it or because you'll never notice it. Both are a heartbreaking waste of a life.

Transforming Dreams into Goals

So, how do you know when your dreams have come true? It's simple: you write them down and keep writing them down, over and over again until they feel part of you; until they become lists of things you're doing every day that take you a step closer to where you want to be. Then you'll have markers. Then you'll know how close you're getting to your dreams. The thing to remember is that a dream may be a wish your heart makes – according to Cinderella – but it's going to stay just that unless you turn it into a *goal*.

Dreams are things that appear unobtainable: they're so far removed from where we are and what we think we're capable of that they seem impossible. But when we turn our dreams into goals they become things to aim for, to plan for, and to set targets for so that we hit them, strike them off and move on to the next one until our dream result is in sight.

That may not sound as romantic as just singing a song and a fairy godmother waving a magic wand, but as I've said, there are no magic wands – at least not in the way you'd imagine.

**YOU are the magic wand.
You're the one who makes
things happen – it just
takes longer, that's all.**

When it comes to setting goals and objectives, making plans and all that kind of thing, there are many great books out there that can help you find a strategy that works for you. Have a look through them; they're all different and it's important to find which one works for you. Some of us like to be self-driven; some need rewards and pats on the back; others don't need anything at all – they can put their head down and are laser-focused on getting what they want!

I'm a mixture of all these things and what I've found works best for me is having a notebook in which to write everything. I jot down ideas, lists, thoughts… some of them good, most of them terrible. I never used to plan anything. I've always worked creatively so when I had a deadline and knew what I needed to do, I worked until I got it done – whether it was writing books or articles, doing research for TV shows, redecorating the kitchen… whatever. My life has usually been a series of short bursts of aiming for things, working towards them, then setting new goals. I've never been without a goal!

Some people like to use daily planners – they're great too, and I do use them, but I still find that most of my planning is done in my head. I don't always need to write it down just to tick it off, if that makes sense. Where I've found planners useful recently, however, is in splitting my goals into sections, so that it's not all about work. At one time, I only set work goals: it never occurred to me that I should be aiming to do anything else right.

I never put down things like 'date night'. Why would I? We'd just grab a free evening when we had one. Surely that's what everyone does, right? Wrong. Couple time needs to be factored in. Actually, you need to make time for everything that's important to you – relationships, family, friends, relaxation, fitness, spirituality. They all need to be catered for.

I only realized this very recently when Nick and I bought planners that made us put aside time for all of these things. We now factor into our diaries family dinner times, salsa classes once a week for the two of us, and reminders to meditate and take time out. I didn't realize how important all of these things are in keeping my work–life balance in check, and how much I'd just been muddling through. These things are vital: let's face it, what's the point of wishing for an amazing partner, for beautiful children, or a fantastic job and then not giving each of these *and* our incredible selves the attention they deserve?

Write lists of what you want to achieve, the goals you want to reach. Each time you tick one off, remember to reward yourself! It's not all about getting the big prize: it's important to enjoy getting there. So don't forget to give yourself a pat on the back – you deserve it.

Dreams will stay as dreams unless you work towards them; no one else is going to do this for you, so you have to get stuck in. Discover something that makes your heart soar, that you love, and find a way to make it work for you. Stick at it. Then keep sticking at it until you get there. Then keep sticking at it to *keep* it. It's as simple as that.

Takeaways to ▶**THRIVE**

▶ Visualizing our future working out in the way we want it to can help us achieve our dreams and goals.

▶ We shouldn't see every obstacle as a reason to stop, or think that we've failed – things just haven't *yet* worked out in the way we want them to.

▶ Things are happening in the order they're supposed to, rather than in the order *we* want them to. We *are* getting there.

▶ Turning our dreams into goals that we can work towards makes the unobtainable perfectly possible.

CHAPTER 10

You Are A Girl On Fire

Throughout this book, I've drawn on my personal life to give you examples of how you can Live, Learn and Thrive in a Life You Love. This is because I've realized the importance of being truly open with you.

Trusting the Universe

My beloved husband, the man I was destined to meet at a time when I was ready to receive him, came into my life when neither of us was looking for love. We were both in a pretty dark place and relationships were the last thing on our mind. But we both believe that the universe has a habit of giving you what you need – not what you want – at the time when you need to get it.

Nick and I had agreed to go on a blind date set up by mutual friends. I worked with the woman (Donna, who I've mentioned several times in the book) and Nick played golf with her husband

Dan. It was a double date, to make it less awkward. At that point I'd been divorced for almost two years, and I'd decided that as I obviously had no clue when it came to men, I was staying well clear of them. Nick was in the middle of his divorce and was ill with stress. We were both pretending to the outside world that we were coping, but inside, we were a mess.

I barely looked at Nick for the first half an hour of our date. I let the guys do the talking – they were laughing and joking as men do – while Donna and I chatted quietly. Then, as we all left the bar to go to a local restaurant, Donna and Dan slid away to let Nick and I walk together. Once inside the restaurant and after a few nerve-soothing cocktails, I decided, for some unknown reason, to be completely open with this man I'd never met before. I told him everything about myself.

Everything: including the truth about why I'd been twice divorced. I figured he could just go home and Google me if he wanted to, and that would throw up all kinds of conjecture and half-truths. If he wanted to know the *real* me, then this was it, warts and all, take it or leave it. I had nothing to lose; I didn't even care anymore. Nick was quiet and just listened. He told me later he wasn't simply being a good listener – he was shell-shocked. Was this what dating meant – telling people your darkest secrets right from the off?!

A few hours later we went next door to a nightclub – the first time I'd been to one for years! It was set over three floors and was for people aged from about 30 upwards, so it was pretty chilled, with different music on each floor and places to sit and relax. We all chatted and then headed upstairs to the roof terrace for some fresh air.

On the way back down the dance floor was crowded, and Nick reached out to take my hand and guide me through. The second his hand touched mine we both gasped in shock and stared at each other. A huge electric current had run through us, from our fingertips right through our bodies. We both stood still and stared, seeing each other clearly for the first time. Everything stopped. And then he kissed me...

Forty-five minutes later we came up for air.

At this point I need to stress that I'm *not* the kind of lady who kisses men I barely know in the middle of nightclubs. I kind of wish I was because it would make me a whole lot more exciting. I'd also have much better stories to tell at dinner parties. But I'm not. That isn't the kind of thing I do! What I did next should have felt insane, but it didn't – it felt completely natural and right. I asked Nick to take me home. So he did. Donna and Dan raised an eyebrow or two and laughed as we headed out into the street. I went back to Nick's flat and, well, the rest as they say, is history.

Doing What's Best for Us

The reason I'm telling *you* this (even though I haven't told my mum – sorry, Mum! Or my dad: yup, I did everything you're *not* supposed to do) is because sometimes you just have to do what feels right. Even if it's completely out of character. Sometimes you really do have to say 'fuck it' and let the universe, as Gabrielle Bernstein would say, 'have your back'.

Now, that doesn't mean dashing off to bed with every guy you kiss in a nightclub! But when you feel a genuine connection with someone or something – whether it's a bold career move or the colour you want to paint your bathroom – *just do it*.

Nick and I have spoken about this so many times since we got together. There were hundreds of reasons why we should have split up after that one night, and very few why we should have stayed together. We lived in different counties, so it meant almost an hour's drive each time we wanted to see each other. He was in a mess: he was depressed and seeing a counsellor every week.

He'd also been diagnosed with a heart condition and was waiting to hear if he'd need surgery. In the meantime he kept blacking out; I once got a phone call from a policeman asking if I knew the person who'd called me from a certain mobile. Nick had been found slumped unconscious on a bench when he was supposed to be at a work event three hours away from where I lived. Apparently he'd felt unwell and must have taken himself outside – he couldn't remember. The police didn't know how long he'd been there – people had thought he was drunk and kept walking by. I drove at night to collect him from the hospital, shocked and worried.

Emotionally, he still kept me at arm's length. He felt it was too soon to get involved with someone, so I was just there for him and cared about him. He'd lost his business, his home and his health, all in one year. He'd literally had to pick himself up and start all over again.

> **Sometimes there are bigger forces at play, and we just have to trust that everything's happening for a reason.**

Through his three years of therapy Nick vowed that he'd come out of his situation a better man. He vowed that he wouldn't repeat the mistakes he'd made in his personal life; that he'd be a better partner and father. He works on himself daily: I've never known anyone as committed to being better every day than him. Nick and I do things in our own way; we try to be good people, to guide our children to be good people, to do the right thing.

Neither of us is perfect, but we're a helluva lot better than we were when we first met! We believe in each other – we see things in each other that I genuinely believe no one else has seen before – and this makes us braver, more daring, more willing to dream big and push for great things. I think we've both always had this inside of us. We've both said that when we were young we felt we were destined to do great things – we just didn't know what they were. Now we do: we work together on our website to help every woman feel stronger, braver, more equipped than they've ever been to live the life they were destined to live.

All of our experiences have brought us to this place, and everything we've learned through all the people we've met along the way, we pass on. I truly believe that we were destined to meet, that the universe was waiting until we were ready. I believe that I had to go through everything I did to get me to the place I am now because if I hadn't, I wouldn't be as committed as I am to helping others. I feel passionately grateful that I was with someone who loved me enough to let me fall when I needed to and helped me back on my feet again, so that I can carry on, stronger than before.

Don't get me wrong: our lives together aren't all rose-tinted! There are times when we drive each other insane – when we get angry, irritated, oversensitive, sulky, petulant: all the good stuff! We have a blended family and on the whole, that works wonderfully: the kids genuinely get on and love each other. However, having four teenagers coming and going into homes with different boundaries, rules and behaviours is challenging. Some nights when we lie in bed doing our daily 'What are you grateful for?' routine, the simple answer is: 'I'm grateful that today is finally over and I can start again tomorrow.'

Positivity in the Face of Adversity

So, this is what I'm getting at. You can't always change your circumstances right away. You can't wave a magic wand and make everything the way you want it. But you *can* take steps, make decisions, and then move out of the way and let the things happen the way they're meant to happen.

How many times have you looked back and realized that the thing you were really hoping for, *really* pushing for, and were so disappointed when it didn't work out the way you wanted, *actually* worked out for the best in the end? So many!

My granny's favourite saying was: 'What's for you won't go by you' and she was absolutely right. If it's meant to be, it'll happen. Have your dreams, make your plans, keep working, but let things pan out – don't try to force them into a shape that you've decided fits.

I heard a great quote on Lewis Howes' 'The School of Greatness' podcast from an American rapper called Prince Ea. He said: 'When we argue with reality, we lose.' Wow, that's profound – and so simple! There's absolutely no point in bemoaning the way things are unless you're prepared to do something about it that changes your life for the better. Everything that should have happened has happened.

We have to live in the now and create an acceptance of what is, but that doesn't mean it can't improve and be better. This is what it means to Live, Learn and Thrive in a Life You Love – learning from each experience, figuring out how to take that learning and move forwards, all whilst loving the journey along the way.

Deep down we know that it's adversity that leads us to great things. I've always believed that we learn the most through our most painful journeys. I believe there has to be a way to take our worst of times and turn it into our best of times. In every case, the outcome is the same – it's how we responded to it that determined the course of our future.

We *choose* whether to be optimistic or not. We *choose* to look on the bright side over the negative side. It doesn't come naturally: we make a choice! It's way easier to do nothing, not to try, not to live in the hope that things will work out, because in doing so we avoid the disappointment that it may not.

But the only alternative to trying is living a life filled with empty bitterness that things haven't worked out the way we wanted and feeling that life is hard and we're powerless to change it. Which to me is a life wasted: a waste of opportunity and a waste of our healthy state, all of it.

There's always something to be optimistic about. Even when life is challenging, we can focus on what's working and going right.

The very act of looking positively on your circumstances means you're able to see opportunities that you'd have missed if you were buried neck-deep in misery and pessimism, with your head down and your eyes and ears closed to anything other than how terrible things are.

It's like the blue car analogy – if you're constantly on the lookout for a blue car, eventually you're going to spot them everywhere. So make sure that the blue car in your life is something positive, not negative, because you'll always find what you're searching for, even if you didn't realize you were looking.

Just think about the kind of energy you give off when you're angry, disillusioned and pissed off with life. It's not good is it? And who wants to be around someone who's giving off energy like this? No one.

I know this first-hand from when I was feeling at my lowest before my breakdown; from the time when I felt that everyone was against me, that people were being deliberately mean and unhelpful, that opportunities I'd worked for weren't panning out. I was so focused on all the things that weren't working out that I couldn't see the things that were.

Get Ready to Reset

Millions of people had their own unique experience of the virus pandemic that swept across the globe in 2020. When the spread of coronavirus disease (Covid-19) reached biblical proportions and whole countries went into lockdown, none of us could have known how we'd react. I'd always joked with my children that they were on their own if a zombie apocalypse ever happened because zombies scare the hell out of me. I can't watch alien invasion movies because I think I'd be the one panicking and making all the wrong decisions.

And yet, when coronavirus struck, really struck, and my live TV show was taken off air, the kids were sent home from school, and all we had was each other, I didn't think about myself at all. My mission became to survive it: to make sure our unit stayed indoors, stayed safe, had enough food, and kept to a routine that gave us goals to check off every day. To make sure that we exercised, played games, and had reasons to feel that we'd achieved something, that we were succeeding on our own level.

I didn't know that this would be my reaction. None of us know until we're put in an impossible situation. Feeling fear, real fear, on a scale not experienced by generations before ours, brought out instincts in all of us – some of them better than others. If there's one thing we can take away from the global fear we've experienced, it's that our old fears don't matter as much as we thought they did. The worry about failing, about embarrassing ourselves, getting it wrong… all those things that go through our mind when life is 'normal' don't mean anything now. So dump them. Get rid of them.

At the time of writing, I don't know how the world is going to come out the other side of the coronavirus pandemic. My hope is that it'll leave us all with a deep appreciation for the simple pleasures in life that we all took for granted. For me, it's Sunday lunch with my elderly parents, from whom we've had to stay away for their protection; friends coming over; hugging people we love; and travelling to beautiful places.

Before these things were taken away from us they were so much a part of our lives that it was impossible to imagine them not being there. How we move forwards from surviving this global experience is down to each one of us, literally down to each individual. Just as it was at the outset of the crisis, when we were told to observe social distancing and thousands selfishly didn't. As it was when we were told to stay away from elderly loved ones to protect them, and some did and some didn't.

Our future depends on our present. How you behave right now, in this moment, defines how the rest of your life will be.

Learn from your mistakes – they're all in the past now. This is a time for new beginnings, for fresh starts.

The slate has been wiped clean and we're ready to begin again. The legend of the phoenix tells that this beautiful, immortal creature burst into flames at the end of its life, only to be reborn from its ashes to live once again. It has come to symbolize many things: rebirth, immortality and life after death to name just a few. To me, it symbolizes the way that we've always, since the beginning of time, experienced our own new beginnings.

We've all been through experiences in which the 'old' us has been left behind, or laid to rest, and the 'new' us emerges. It can come in so many ways: simply becoming an adolescent and leaving childhood behind is a slow rebirth; the transformation into adulthood and everything it brings is another.

But our transformations, our rebirths, don't end there. We're constantly evolving and changing, and it's always in times of pressure that we grow the most. As a society on planet Earth we've experienced pressures that have touched each and every one of us: as individuals, as families, as colleagues, as friends. As women, our perspective on what it means to be a 'Girl on Fire' has changed, with each of us defining success in our own personal way. For some this has been an opportunity to dig deep within, to learn, to grow.

What you do with that experience, how you move forwards now, is up to you. Your life experience is different to everyone else's – all our lives are different. *You* are different! And that's what makes you so special.

You've already overcome so much. You're ready to be reborn, to start again. So get excited. Feel the joy. Write the list. Do the work. Keep doing the work. And keep going until each little box has been ticked, each little goal has been reached. And once you get to that goal, you'll be so on fire you'll write yourself a new goal and just keep going. How do I know this? Because that's what Girls on Fire *do*.

And *You*. Are. On. Fire.

Recommended Reading

Below is a list of the books from which I've learned so much on my journey to becoming a Girl on Fire. I recommend you dive into them to study their wisdom and use it to help you along your own path to everything you dream of and more!

Gabrielle Bernstein, *The Universe Has Your Back*; Hay House UK, 2016

Pete Cohen, *Inspirators: Leading The Way In Leadership*; Filament Publishing, 2019

Pete Cohen, Bobby Cappuccio, *Shut The Duck Up*; Filament Publishing, 2015

Amy Cuddy, *Presence: Bringing Your Boldest Self To Your Biggest Challenges*; Orion, 2016

Camilla Sacre Dallerup, *It's Not You, It's Me*; Watkins Publishing, 2016

Elizabeth Day, *How To Fail: Everything I've Ever Learned from Things Going Wrong*; Fourth Estate, 2019

Oprah Winfrey, *What I Know For Sure*; Macmillan, 2014

Acknowledgements

This book wouldn't be in your hands without the help of so many people. They say it takes a village to raise a child, and this book has been my baby for the past year. Thank you to everyone who has supported me:

Donna – thank you for being my friend. Carly – you always believed in this book and it would never have got off the ground if it wasn't for you, thank you. To the wonderful team at Hay House – Michelle, Jo, Emily, Lizzi, Tom, Debra, Hannah, Julie, Lucy and Diane – for your belief in me and what I wanted to do, for pulling out all the stops to bring me into your fold and make this happen. I appreciate you and everything you've done, and I hope this is the start of a beautiful thing.

To Gabby Bernstein, Bryony Gordon, Carrie Green, Viv Groskop and Suzy Walker – thank you for your incredible testimonials. I literally danced round the kitchen with excitement to know that you 'got it'!

To my wonderful children, for your patience with me and your love for me. I love you to the moon and back.

To Nick. Thank you for loving me so much that I could finally fall. Thank you for catching me. Thank you for listening, for your kindness, for supporting me, for believing in me. Thank you for the endless cups of coffee, the space and the time to do this. I love you.

And finally, to the weird and wonderful ways of the universe – thank you. I see now that everything is exactly as it should be and always has been. I embrace it all.

ABOUT THE AUTHOR

Nicky Johnston

Andrea McLean is the #1 *Sunday Times* bestselling author of *Confessions of a Good Girl* and *Confessions of a Menopausal Woman*. She is an award-winning TV broadcaster, journalist and radio presenter, and has interviewed some of the biggest names in the entertainment business, including Oprah Winfrey, Drew Barrymore, Will Smith and Amy Schumer.

She is also the CEO and co-founder of the female empowerment site thisgirlisonfire.com. Andrea's mission is to empower 100 million women around the world to Live, Learn and Thrive in a Life they Love.

OfficialTGIOF

@OfficialTGIOF

OfficialTGIOF

www.thisgirlisonfire.com

this girl is on fire ®

This Girl Is On Fire...

for women who want more out of life...
more clarity, direction, energy,
knowledge, fun, money, time, freedom,
control, fulfilment, love.

Why us...

We know we can help you feel great about
yourself, take control, learn new skills and
encourage you to grow into an
unstoppable Girl On Fire. You
really do only get one life... so let's do this!

www.thisgirlisonfire.com

 OfficialTGIOF   OfficialTGIOF   OfficialTGIOF

Live, Learn & Thrive in a life you love

Listen. Learn. Transform.

Listen to the audio version of this book for FREE!

Today, life is more hectic than ever—so you deserve on-demand and on-the-go solutions that inspire growth, center your mind, and support your well-being.

Introducing the *Hay House Unlimited Audio* mobile app. Now you can listen to this book (and countless others)—without having to restructure your day.

With your membership, you can:

- Enjoy over 30,000 hours of audio from your favorite authors.
- Explore audiobooks, meditations, Hay House Radio episodes, podcasts, and more.
- Listen anytime and anywhere with offline listening.
- Access exclusive audios you won't find anywhere else.

Try FREE for 7 days!

Visit hayhouse.com/unlimited to start your free trial and get one step closer to living your best life.

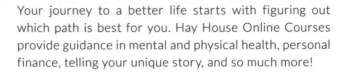

Hay House Podcasts
Bring Fresh, Free Inspiration Each Week!

Hay House proudly offers a selection of life-changing audio content via our most popular podcasts!

Hay House Meditations Podcast

Features your favorite Hay House authors guiding you through meditations designed to help you relax and rejuvenate. Take their words into your soul and cruise through the week!

Dr. Wayne W. Dyer Podcast

Discover the timeless wisdom of Dr. Wayne W. Dyer, world-renowned spiritual teacher and affectionately known as "the father of motivation." Each week brings some of the best selections from the 10-year span of Dr. Dyer's talk show on Hay House Radio.

Hay House Podcast

Enjoy a selection of insightful and inspiring lectures from Hay House Live events, listen to some of the best moments from previous Hay House Radio episodes, and tune in for exclusive interviews and behind-the-scenes audio segments featuring leading experts in the fields of alternative health, self-development, intuitive medicine, success, and more! Get motivated to live your best life possible by subscribing to the free Hay House Podcast.

Find Hay House podcasts on iTunes, or visit www.HayHouse.com/podcasts for more info.

HAY HOUSE

Look within

Join the conversation about latest products,
events, exclusive offers and more.

 Hay House

 @HayHouseUK

 @hayhouseuk

 healyourlife.com

We'd love to hear from you!